St Andrews
& Fife
Walks

St Andrews
& *Fife*
Walks

Campbell Brown & Steven Wiggins

B&W PUBLISHING • EDINBURGH

Copyright © Campbell Brown & Steven Wiggins 1992

All rights reserved.
No part of this publication may be reproduced
in any form or by any means without the
prior permission of the publishers,
B&W Publishing, 7 Sciennes, Edinburgh EH9 1NH.

ISBN 0 9515151 2 8

British Library Cataloguing in Publication Data:
A catalogue record for this book is available
from the British Library.

Other titles available:

Edinburgh Walks Volume One
ISBN 0 9515151 7 9

Edinburgh Walks Volume Two
The Pentlands & The Lothians
ISBN 0 9515151 3 6

Glasgow Walks
ISBN 0 9515151 1 X

Printed by Redwood Press Ltd

Contents

1   The Castle to the West Sands   1

2   The Cathedral to the Long Pier   18

3   The University Walk   36

4   South Street and St Mary's   48

5   Lade Braes   59

6   The Old Course   63

7   East Sands to Kingsbarns   70

8   Magus Muir   74

9   Crail to Fife Ness   81

10   Anstruther and Cellardyke   94

11   Kilrenny   111

12   Pittenweem   117

13   St Monans Church to Newark Castle   126

14   Elie: The Town & the Beach   134

15   Earlsferry: The Chain Walk   138

16   Upper Largo to Lower Largo   143

17   Earlshall Castle and Leuchars   155

18   Falkland   162

19   East Lomond and West Lomond   172

20   Hill of Tarvit   177

21   Dairsie Castle and Riverside Walk   184

22   The Isle of May   188

Photographs by Steven Wiggins

Acknowledgements

The authors would like to thank:
- Anna for invaluable research assistance at Pittenweem
- The Graphics Company (031-225 7232) for their generous technical advice and expertise
- Harry S Palmer for cartographic services rendered

Introduction

The main thing to remember when walking in the countryside is to use common sense, both in the equipment you take with you and the way you treat the environment. Much of the land you pass through is privately owned farmland and a few basic rules should be followed:

- keep to rights of way whenever possible,
- avoid fields under cultivation,
- avoid creating disturbances during the lambing season from March to June, and take special care to ensure that dogs are kept under control.

We have made every effort to ensure that the information in this book is accurate. However, the inclusion of a walk in this guide does not necessarily guarantee access and it up to the walker, if in doubt, to check that the route is still open. Because the countryside is not a static environment, conditions may well alter as time goes on, but intelligent use of the recommended maps should overcome any such difficulties.

After Constantinople and Naples,
the finest prospect in Europe.
Boswell *on Fife*

I did not come to Fife to get a good
dinner, but to see savage men and
savage manners, and I have not
been disappointed.
Dr Johnson

THE CASTLE TO THE WEST SANDS

The Castle
Mine and Countermine
St Salvators Quad
Sea Life Centre
Martyrs Monument
Royal and Ancient
British Golf Museum
West Sands

Starting Point: St Andrews Castle
at the east end of The Scores

Opening Times
St Andrews Castle: Summer—9.30am-6pm
For winter opening, check with the tourist
information office (0334 72021)

British Golf Museum: Summer—10am-5.30pm
For winter opening, check with the museum
(0334 78880)

Recommended Maps
St Andrews Street Plan (4th Edition)
Ordnance Survey Landranger 59

Distance: 1 mile (excluding West Sands)

Tearooms
Crumbs Pavilion Tearoom
The Scores Hotel

The first castle to stand on this site was built by **Bishop Roger De Beaumont** around 1200, but very little remains of his work and the buildings that still stand mostly date from the 16th century—350 turbulent years ensured that the castle was constantly being rebuilt. From the late 15th century until 1560 this was the residence of the Bishops of St Andrews, and its history is inextricably linked to the intrigue that surrounded these men.

The castle changed hands many times during the 14th century Wars of Independence between the English and the Scots, being virtually destroyed in the siege of 1337, before being rebuilt by **Bishop Walter Traill** in 1385. The castle was also closely associated with the Scottish Crown—**James I** was educated here by Bishop Wardlaw, **James II** lived here for a time and **James III** may well have been born here in 1451. It is worth noting that these were three of the least fortunate of Scotland's monarchs: James I was assassinated at Perth in 1437, James II was killed at Floors Castle near Roxburgh in 1460 when one of his own artillery pieces exploded, and James III was murdered in mysterious circumstances after falling from his horse at the Battle of Sauchieburn in 1488. The ill-fortune did not end there; **James IV**, the chivalrous renaissance monarch, was killed at Flodden Field in 1513 and his son, Archbishop Alexander Stewart of St Andrews, died with him *(see Walk 2—The Cathedral).*

The heyday of the castle came during the time of **Archbishop James Beaton** (1523-39) and his nephew, **Cardinal David Beaton** (1539-46), who succeeded him. In James Beaton's day the castle was renowned as one of the most convivial houses in Scotland, and this reputation continued during the time of his nephew, who was extending the castle when fate overtook him and brought the great period of the castle's history to an end.

Cardinal David Beaton (1494-1546) had studied in Scotland and on the continent before becoming a Bishop in France in 1537 and a Cardinal in 1538. He was Chancellor in the government of the **Earl of Arran** (1516-1575) from 1543. Like many prelates of his time, Beaton was more of a worldly politician than a priest, and the fact that he had several illegitimate children and a mistress was exactly the sort of thing the Lutheran reformers despised about the state of the Church in the 16th century. **John Winram**, the saintly sub-prior of St Andrews, no doubt had Beaton in mind when he preached at the trial of George Wishart that:

> 'A Bishop must be faultless, not
> stubborn, not angry, no drunkard,
> no fighter, not given to filthy lucre.'

Beaton ran into trouble when he opposed Henry VIII's plans to marry off his young son and heir, Edward, to the infant daughter of James V—the future **Mary Queen of Scots**. In 1543 **Henry VIII** declared war on Scotland over this issue and the ensuing period became known as **'The Rough Wooing'**, with the English forces under the command of the Earl of Hertford laying waste to large areas of eastern Scotland.

Although St Andrews was not touched, a fact that has been attributed to a certain amount of astute bribery of the English by Beaton, a so-called 'English faction' arose in St Andrews in support of Henry VIII, and prominent among them was **George**

Wishart (1513-46), a Protestant reformer who counted John Knox amongst his followers.

Wishart was a learned man and a powerful preacher who had left Scotland to study in Germany, Switzerland and at Cambridge University, before returning to Scotland in 1543. It has been suggested that Wishart may even have been an agent of the English Crown, but, whatever the truth of that, Beaton certainly saw him as a dangerous adversary and took action against him. Wishart was arrested at Haddington in East Lothian, imprisoned and tried for heresy.

The trial took place in St Andrews Cathedral on 28th February 1546. Beaton was present, as well as the Bishop of Glasgow and a large number of clergy and men at arms. Standing in the pulpit, Wishart told the assembled clergy that he had done nothing other than preach the word of God; but the clergy clearly feared that his powers of persuasion and command of scripture would turn the people against them. A quick trial followed by a summary execution was the only possible outcome. After being condemned as a heretic, Wishart was taken to the castle to await execution.

The next day a fire was built up outside the castle, and Wishart was led out, bound and chained, with bags of gunpowder tied to him. Beaton and others sat on cushions high on the castle wallhead to get the best view of the proceedings. Wishart addressed the people:

> 'I suffer this day by men, not
> sorrowfully, but with a glad heart and
> mind. For this cause was I sent, that I

should suffer this fire for Christ's sake.
Consider and behold my visage, ye
shall not see me change my colour.'

Wishart was then placed in the fire and was killed by a combination of burning, strangulation and the explosion of the gunpowder. But before the rope was tightened around his neck, he had time to say this of Cardinal Beaton:

'God forgive yon man that lies so
glorious on yon wall head; but within
few days he shall lie as shamfull as he
lies glorious now.'

The prophecy was soon fulfilled, as the execution of Wishart was the final straw for Beaton's Protestant enemies in St Andrews.

In May 1546 a number of conspirators, led by **Sir William Kirkcaldy of Grange** (1520-73), managed to break into the castle while rebuilding work was being carried out. According to Knox's account, they met little resistance from the Cardinal's men, and once in Beaton's chamber one of their number, **James Melville**, took the trouble to explain to the Cardinal that they had come to carry out the 'work and judgement of God':

'For heir before my God I protest that
neither hatrent of thy person, the luif of
thy riches, nor the fear of any truble
thow could have done to me in
particulare, moved, nor moves me to
stryk thee; but only becaus thow hast
bein, and remanes ane obstinat
ennemye against Christ Jesus and His
holy evangell.'

Melville then ran Beaton through several times with his sword. Beaton's last words were 'I am a priest! I am a priest! Fy, Fy, all is gone.' His body was later hung from the top of the castle wall above the entrance, before being pickled in salt, deposited in the bottle dungeon of the castle, and eventually buried in Blackfriars Chapel.

This Protestant faction, or **'The Castilians'** as they were known, was able to hold the castle for a year, with some assistance from Henry VIII, until the Earl of Arran and a French fleet commanded by the **Prior of Capua** recaptured the castle in July 1547. The initial siege had only lasted from September to December of 1546. With the Castilians holding Arran's young son hostage, Arran does not seem to have been too keen to press home the siege, and an outbreak of plague gave him an excuse to begin negotiations. There was even talk of Papal absolution for the murder of Beaton, and things rapidly quietened down. However, shortly after **John Knox** joined the Castilians, a French fleet sailed into St Andrews Bay in June 1547.

The Castilians were now up against a much more determined and professional opponent, **Leone Strozzi, the Prior of Capua**, an expert in the use of artillery. Strozzi mounted guns on the walls of the cathedral and the tower of St Salvator's and, at first light on the 30th July, the bombardment of the castle began. The walls were quickly breached and Sir William Kirkcaldy, who commanded the Castilians, surrendered the castle. John Knox was one of those captured and spent almost two years as a galley slave in the French fleet.

Sir William Kirkcaldy of Grange, 'a stout man, who always offered by single combat and at point of sword to maintain whatever he said', was also captured and shared Knox's fate, before distinguishing himself as a soldier on the continent and returning to Scotland to resume one of the most colourful careers of the 16th century. He was a deadly enemy of Bothwell, whom he challenged to single combat at **Carberry Hill** and then pursued, unsuccessfully, to Norway.

> 'The honour of a soldier in those days was not deemed incompatible with a change of side as frequent as that of a politician. Though a soldier of fortune, Kirkcaldy had the interest of his country as he saw it as his chief aim.'
> **J. G. Mackay**
> *A History of Fife and Kinross* (1895)

As a result of his bravery at the battle of Langside, Sir William Kirkcaldy was made Governor of Edinburgh Castle. He then made a fatal mistake, going over to Mary Queen of Scots side, and in 1573 he was forced to surrender Edinburgh Castle to Regent Morton's forces. He was tried, condemned and hanged for treason on 3rd August 1573, despite offers of ransom and the desperate attempts of Lord Ruthven and others to save him.

Beaton was succeeded by **Archbishop John Hamilton** (1549-71), half brother of The Earl of Arran and previously Bishop of Dunkeld. Mary Queen of Scots called him 'that poxy priest', and his reputation, like Beaton's, was that of a worldly rather than a spiritual prelate. Hamilton was to be the last Archbishop of St Andrews before the Reformation. His work in rebuilding the castle is commemorated by his crest—the cinquefoil or five-pointed star—that can still be seen over the entrance. After Hamilton's time the castle declined in importance and by the middle of the 17th century it was a ruin whose stone and timbers were being plundered for use in the rebuilding of the harbour walls. In 1801 the East Range of the castle collapsed and fell into the sea when the cliff beneath it gave way.

The present entrance (c.1555) to the castle **(1)** is not the original one; that was in the 14th century **Tower (2)** to your right as you go into the castle, and even this later entrance is not in its original harled state. Just inside the entrance, in the vaulted chambers to the right and left, you will see two of the false starts to the countermining work carried out by the defenders in the siege of 1546-7.

> *Turn left towards the remains of the early 16th century* **Blockhouse** *(3) at the south west corner of the castle.*

This was one of the largest blockhouses in Scotland and there was originally a similar one at the south east corner of the castle; but both of these were destroyed in the siege of 1547. From here you can go up to the South Range, which was the site of Archbishop Hamilton's apartments—the steps at the east end lead down into the **Fore Tower**, the original entrance to the castle. Descending from the South Range, walk across the courtyard to the 14th century **Sea Tower (4)** at the north west corner of the castle.

The lower chamber to the east, reached by a short flight of steps, is the infamous **Bottle Dungeon (5)**—a damp, gloomy, windowless bottle-shaped

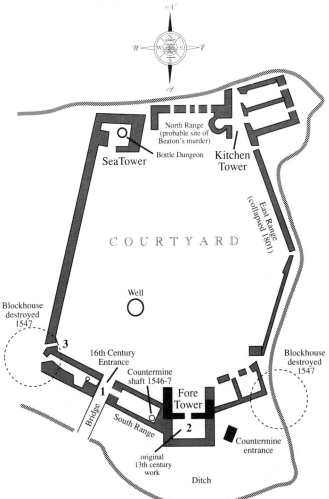

St Andrews Castle

North Range
(probable site of
Beaton's murder)

SeaTower   Bottle Dungeon

Kitchen
Tower

East Range
(collapsed 1801)

COURTYARD

Well

Blockhouse
destroyed
1547

3

16th Century
Entrance

Countermine
shaft 1546-7

Fore
Tower

1

Bridge

South Range

2

original
13th century
work

Blockhouse
destroyed
1547

Countermine
entrance

Ditch

pit prison. Other examples of the medieval pit prison can be seen in ruined castles throughout East Lothian, but this one is particularly unpleasant, having been hollowed out of the rock, and with only a single circular entrance at the top through which prisoners would be dropped onto the stone floor 24 feet below. George Wishart and many others were held here; some are reputed to have been murdered in the dungeon itself.

*After visiting the north range and the kitchen tower at the north east corner, walk across the courtyard to the entrance to the **Countermine (6)** to the east of the **Fore Tower**.*

The Countermine is one of the most unusual and striking features of St Andrews Castle, providing a rare insight into one of the less well known aspects of medieval warfare.

During the siege of 1546-7, the Earl of Arran set about undermining the Fore Tower by means of a tunnel cut through the rock. This was intended to breach the castle defences and allow the besiegers to take the defenders by surprise, possibly breaking into the castle in several places at the same time. However, the castle's defenders realised what was going on and, once they had discovered where the mine was being sunk, began to dig their own countermine and eventually broke into the attackers mine. After this, the attackers relied on the guns of the French Fleet to bring about the castle's surrender in 1547.

Once inside the countermine, by following its low and slanting course, (it is only about 4 feet high) out from the castle, you can see the point (marked by the modern iron ladder) where the defenders broke through into the much larger chamber of the mine. At the furthest extremity of the remaining section of the mine, you are directly underneath the road outside the castle, quite close to where it was originally begun during the siege.

As you leave the castle you can see the stones set into the road that mark the site of George Wishart's execution. These were placed here to commemorate the 400th anniversary of Wishart's death.

Turn right onto The Scores and head west towards St Salvator's and the university buildings.

The Scores is predominantly a Victorian development—before the 19th century there were very few buildings in this part of the town—and there are some fine examples of Scots Baronial style houses, such as Castlecliffe and the aptly-named Edgecliffe, facing the sea.

Walk past the back of St Salvator's Hall of Residence on the left, continue on, and turn left up Butts Wynd. Enter St Salvator's Quadrangle through the gate in the wall on your left.

The Quadrangle (7) was completely rebuilt in the first half of the 19th century by **Robert Reid**, who was responsible for the east side, and **William Nixon** who constructed the north side in 1845-6. Reminiscent of Oxbridge colleges, the 'Quad', as it is known to students, is the site of the anarchic festivities that take place annually on **'Raisin Monday'**. *(For more on St Salvator's Quad & Chapel see The University Walk.)*

St Salvators was founded in 1450 by **Bishop James Kennedy**. The massive tower of the chapel dates from the 1460's, although the spire was a later addition by **Archbishop John Hamilton** in 1550. At the south west corner of the Quad is the Porter's Lodge and Hebdomadar's Building (15th century, rebuilt in the 17th century). In the 17th century the Hebdomadar was in charge of student discipline, checking, amongst other things, that lights were out at 9pm.

The Geography Department is on the east side, and the north side houses lecture rooms, as well as Upper and Lower College Halls—the site of many final examination dramas.

*Leave the Quad by the same gate, and turn right down Butts Wynd to rejoin The Scores. Turn left and head west again along The Scores, passing the modern **University Library (8)** on the left, built in the early 1970's. Passing St James RC church on your right, continue along The Scores to **The Sea Life Centre (9)**.*

The Sea Life Centre is a fairly recent addition to The Scores, housing an extensive collection of fish in a series of imaginatively designed tanks—everything from the humble cod to exotic trigger fish and conger eels. The rays and flatfish in the first room are particularly interesting. Outside the centre there is a seal pool.

*From the Sea Life Centre continue along to the **Martyrs Monument (10)** obelisk.*

Designed by **William Nixon** and placed here in 1842, the Martyrs Monument commemorates those Protestants who were executed for their faith in St

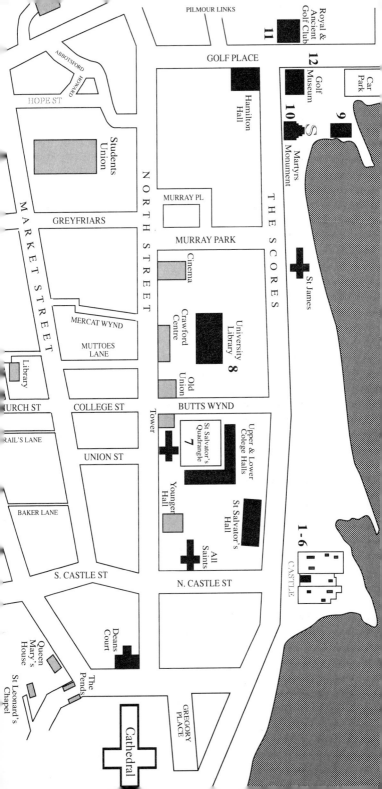

Andrews in the years before the Reformation. They were **Paul Craw** (1433), **Patrick Hamilton** (1528), **Henry Forrest** (1533), **George Wishart** (1546) and **Walter Myln** (1558).

Paul Craw came from Bohemia and was burned because he was a follower of the heretical doctrines of John Hus. Patrick Hamilton was a young aristocrat who had studied at Paris and Louvain and had been influenced by Luther. On his return to St Andrews he began to preach these heretical reformed doctrines. He was soon arrested, tried in the cathedral, and condemned. He was burned at the stake outside St Salvators Chapel on 29th February 1528.

> 'if ye will burn them, let them be burnt
> in deep cellars, for the reek of Master
> Patrick Hamilton has infected as many
> as it blew upon.'

Walter Myln was 82 years old when he was burned by Archbishop Hamilton in 1558. His crime had been to speak in favour of married clergy and against the corruption that characterised medieval pilgrimages. His execution was so unpopular that local people would have no part in it and they built a cairn of stones on the spot where he was burned, just to the west of the castle, to show their disapproval. Henry Forrest was executed simply because he owned a copy of the New Testament in English.

The sea area just to the east was known as **'Witch Lake'**, because suspected witches were thrown into the sea here to test whether or not they were guilty of witchcraft. If the suspect floated, they were guilty; if they sank and drowned, they were inno-

IN
MEMORY OF
THE MARTYRS
PATRICK HAMILTON
HENRY FORREST
GEORGE WISHART
WALTER MILL

WHO
IN SUPPORT OF
THE PROTESTANT FAITH
SUFFERED

DEATH BY FIRE
AT
STANDREWS
BETWEEN THE YEARS

MDXXVIII — MDLVIII
The righteous shall be in everlasting
remembrance

The Martyrs Monument

The West Sands

cent. John Knox himself supervised the condemnation and burning of a 'witch' in St Andrews in the 1570's, and the gullibility of the populace with regard to such dubious accusations did not finally run out until the late 1660's.

Just across Golf Place is the headquarters of the **Royal and Ancient Golf Club (11)**, undoubtedly the most famous golf club in the world. A two storey mid-Victorian villa, it was begun in 1853 and additions were still being made in 1900. It overlooks the first tee of the **Old Course**, which is a regular host of the British Open Golf Championship. Opposite the R&A is the **British Golf Museum (12)**. *(See The Old Course Walk for details.)*

Right on the corner of Golf Place and The Scores is **Hamilton Hall**, one of the university Halls of Residence, named after the 14th Duke of Hamilton. Built in 1895 as the Grand Hotel, it is a well known local landmark with its unusual bell-shaped tower.

This walk can be continued by turning right down Golf Place, then left along the Bruce Embankment and onto the West Sands. This is one of the finest stretches of beach in Scotland, and was used as a location during the filming of 'Chariots Of Fire'.

2

THE CATHEDRAL TO THE LONG PIER

Deans Court
Nave
South Transept
Cloister
Chapter House
Museum
St Rule's Tower
Haunted Tower
St Mary's Church of The Rock
The Long Pier
The Pends

Starting Point: Deans Court
opposite the Cathedral.

Opening Times
Cathedral: Summer 9.30am-6pm
For winter opening, check with the tourist
information office (0334 72021).
Entry to cathedral grounds free.
Entry to The Museum & St Rules Tower £1.

Recommended Maps
St Andrews Street Plan (4th Edition)
Ordnance Survey Landranger 59

Distance: 1 mile

Tearooms
The Merchants House, 49 South Street
Ladyhead Bookshop & Coffeeshop, North St

This walk begins outside **Deans Court (1)**, and before moving into the precincts of the cathedral itself it is well worth having a look at Deans Court. Although the building only dates from the 16th century, the courtyard, with its ancient looking well gives the place an air of much greater antiquity. The gates that lead into the courtyard date from the early 1930's, when Deans Court was converted into a university Hall of Residence.

> *Cross the road and enter the cathedral through the*
> ***West Front arch (2).***

St Andrews Cathedral was built close to where **St Rule** is said to have landed in the 8th century AD. Although there is some doubt as to whether Rule ever existed, he apparently came from Greece and brought with him a selection of relics of St Andrew, including a kneecap, three fingers and a tooth.

Several churches were soon built, and a shrine to **St Andrew** was established. In the first half of the 12th century **St Rule's Church**, the tower and choir of which can still be seen today, was built to house the relics of St Andrew, and its administration was shared between the original Celtic or 'Culdee' clergy and the Augustinians, who came to St Andrews in the 1120's. Gradually, the Culdees were eased out— by the 1140's there were less than 20 of them left— and they took up residence in the Church of St Mary of the Rock, the ruins of which can be seen on the cliffs to the east of the cathedral.

The cathedral was built to replace St Rule's between 1160 and 1318—which may seem rather a long time, but this was a massive undertaking, and it was to be the largest cathedral in Scotland. The founder of the cathedral was **Arnold, Abbot of Kelso**, but it was not completed until the time of **Bishop William Lamberton**, who carried out the consecration on 5th July 1318 in the presence of **Robert the Bruce**.

The building work was begun at the east end, as this enabled the choir to be brought into use as soon as possible, long before the rest of the building was completed. As a result the 12th century eastern end of the cathedral was built in the Romanesque style, while the western end reflects the development of the Gothic style in the 13th century.

The design of the cathedral included a nave with twelve bays, a central tower over the crossing, north and south transepts, and a six bay choir. To the south of the cathedral itself were the buildings of the Augustinian Priory, grouped around the cloister. These included living accommodation for the friars and administrative buildings such as the Chapter House (built by Bishop Lamberton at the start of the 14th century).

In the 14th century the whole of the cathedral precinct was surrounded by a massive defensive wall over half a mile in length and 20 feet high in places, which was rebuilt in the 1520's by **Prior John Hepburn** and his successor **Patrick Hepburn**. The Hepburns added the defensive towers, 16 of which were still standing at the end of the 17th century, although only 13 remain today.

In 1280 the original West Front of the cathedral fell down during a storm and was rebuilt by Bishop Wishart. Another disaster occurred in 1378, when a fire destroyed much of the cathedral, and the repairs were not completed until 1440. In 1409 the south transept gable end also fell down during a storm. Little further damage occurred before the Reformation, although the central tower was apparently giving cause for concern by the mid-16th century.

In June 1559 a mob encouraged by the preaching of **John Knox** entered the cathedral and caused great damage, looting everything of value—including the contents of the Bishops tombs. The building then gradually fell into ruin, after the removal of its lead roofing and the collapse of the central tower towards the end of the 16th century. As had happened with the castle, the cathedral soon became little more than a convenient source of building materials for the people of the town. Very little was done to remedy this state of affairs until the end of the 19th century.

The remains of the **West Front** of the cathedral that you see today are the result of late 13th century work and the post-1378 repairs. After the collapse of 1280, the West Front was rebuilt a little to the east of its original position, thus shortening the nave by about 30 feet. Above the arcading that still survives there would originally have been two tiers, each with twin Gothic windows. Fragments of the tracery that decorated these windows can still be seen. Just inside the West Front, set into the north wall of the nave is a tomb, probably that of a Bishop.

Moving into the main body of the cathedral you enter the **Nave** *(3).*

Little remains of the Nave except the south wall and the bases of four of the original pillars. You may notice that the first six bays at the west end have Gothic windows, while the last four bays to the east have round-arched Romanesque windows. The explanation for this is that the Gothic windows date from one of the 13th or 14th century rebuilding phases, and the Romanesque windows are from the original building work of the 12th century.

Continuing eastwards along the Nave you pass the well and go through the Crossing, between the North and South Transepts, above which stood the tower.

Very little remains of the **North Transept (4)**, but some of the 12th century work remains in the **South Transept (5),** along with fragments of the Romanesque arcading and a number of tombstones.

To the west of the South Transept is the **Cloister (6)**, surrounded by the remains of the Priory's 13th century domestic buildings. To the south east is the site of the **Chapter House (7)**, with the old Chapter House just to the west. The second Chapter House dates from the early 14th century and its south wall still has the stone seating that was in use in Bishop Lamberton's time.

St Andrews Cathedral

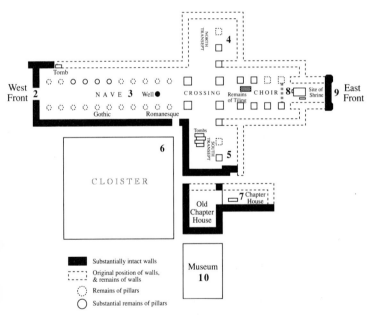

NORTH TRANSEPT

4

West Front

2

Tomb

NAVE **3** Well ●

Gothic Romanesque

CROSSING Remains of Tiling C H O I R **8** Site of Shrine **9** East Front

Tombs

SOUTH TRANSEPT

5

CLOISTER

6

Old Chapter House

7 Chapter House

Museum

10

■ Substantially intact walls

⌐ ⌐ Original position of walls,
        & remains of walls

○ Remains of pillars

◯ Substantial remains of pillars

The Chapter House was the administrative centre of the Priory and it was here that the founding charter of the university was drawn up in February 1412. The Chapter House was also the burial place for the Priors, who were buried under its floor. The stone coffins that can still be seen were probably those of the clerics **John of Forfar** (d.1321), **John of Gowry** (d.1340), **William of Lothian** (d.1354), **Robert of Montrose** (d.1393), and **James Bisset** (d.1416).

Return to the Crossing and turn right into the Choir.

To your left, under a protective wooden cover, there is a reconstructed section of the tiled floor of the cathedral, while to the right are the remains of the lower sections of several pillars. Directly ahead is the Sanctuary, in the shadow of the East Front of the cathedral. This is where the shrine of St Andrew would have been, although no trace of it remains. The massive **Tournai marble slab (8)** that rests here on a number of stone tombs may have been from the tomb of **Archbishop James Stewart** (1480-1504), the brother of **James IV**. The tombs below the marble slab were discovered when excavations were carried out in the early 19th century, as was a skull reputed to have been that of **Alexander Stewart** 'The boy Archbishop' who was killed at the Battle of Flodden in 1513.

Alexander Stewart had been sent to Italy by his father James IV to be taught by **Erasmus**, who thought him an exceptionally gifted student whose 'whole time was given to study, with the exception of what was devoted to religious services or to sleep'. He returned to Scotland, only to die at Flodden along with his father and most of Scotland's nobility, including 13 Earls, the Bishops of Caithness and of The Isles, The

Chancellor, The Lord Chamberlain, The Lord Lyon, and many Highland Lairds. During excavations in the 1820's, a skeleton with a severe wound to the skull was discovered, and it seems quite possible that these may have been the remains of Alexander Stewart, killed by an English halberdier in Northumberland in 1513.

Many other Bishops were buried within the cathedral, including **Bishop William Wishart** (d.1279), **Bishop Malvoisine** (d.1238), and **Bishop William de Landells** (d.1385), but all their tombs were ransacked at the time of the Reformation and their exact positions are now unknown.

The East Front (9) of the cathedral has survived remarkably well, although its window tracery has largely disappeared. Originally, the East Front had three tiers, each containing three round-arched windows. The lower tier remains, but the upper two tiers were replaced by the present window during the reconstruction work carried out by **Prior Haldenston** in the 1430's. The position of the missing two tiers can still be seen in the stonework of the East Front. There may well have been a rose window above the top tier, but this has completely disappeared along with the triangular section of the gable end that contained it.

Leave the ruins of the cathedral at this point and head over to the museum, which is to the south of the cathedral. The Cathedral Museum (10) is in the old warming house and undercroft.

The museum's collections, housed in the beautifully renovated rib-vaulted undercroft, include the Medieval seals of Priors and Vicar Generals, pictish stones, fragments of arches, ribs and vaulting, and tombstones dating from the 13th to the 17th century. The collection of 17th century tombstones are decorated with all kinds of macabre *Memento Mori*— spades, hour-glasses, and skulls and crossbones. One stone even appears to depict a Mr Punch-like figure leading a dog.

'Reader who on this stone dost cast
thine eye doe not forget the blessed
memory of James Carstairs
to whom God did impart
a candid mind without a double heart'
from the tombstone of
James Carstairs d.1671

'Kings and peasants are equal
in the eyes of death'
from the tombstone of
William Barclay d.1641

One of the museum's most important exhibits is the fragmentary remains of the tomb of **Bishop Henry Wardlaw** (1403-1440), one of the founders of the university. Part of the effigy of the Bishop was discovered in a window lintel in South Street, while the head, found in the precinct wall in 1880, may or may not be part of the same effigy. Wardlaw's tomb would originally have been sited near the high altar of the cathedral.

Coming out of the museum go to ***St Rule's Tower (11)***.

St Rule's Church was probably constructed between 1126 and 1144 by Bishop Robert, who brought in a Northumbrian master mason to carry out the work. Although apparently built in Norman times

to house the relics of St Andrew, the remains of the church display Anglo-Saxon characteristics—especially the massive arches and walls of the choir—that leave the exact origins of the church something of a mystery. One possibility is that the church was founded in the 11th century and Bishop Robert simply extended an already established building. The church was much altered over the years, as the different roof-lines or raggles in the eastern wall of the tower testify.

Inside, in the south wall, is the tomb of **Robert Chambers** (1802-1871), the publisher and author of *Traditions of Edinburgh*.

From the top of the 108 foot high tower, which is reached after a moderately strenuous climb up a winding stairway (allegedly haunted by the ghost of Prior Robert of Montrose), the view of the town, the sea and the surrounding countryside is magnificent.

After leaving St Rule's Tower turn right and head towards the precinct wall. Ahead is a rectangular two storey tower, one of the thirteen remaining fortified towers that can be seen along the precinct wall. This is the **'Haunted Tower'***.*

Dean William T. Linskill, a 19th century St Andrews antiquarian, collected a great many stories and legends relating to this mysterious tower: from the ghost of a 'White Lady' who was said to roam the walls in the vicinity, to the strange discoveries made by other antiquarians who originally opened the tower in September 1868. This is the account given to Linskill by Mr Jesse Hall, one of those present in 1868:

'Mr Smith, watchmaker, and Mr Walker, the University Librarian, who were both antiquaries, pressed me frequently to allow them to open the vault. I did not care about it, as I did not like to disturb the dead; but I at last consented, and early one summer morning before six o'clock—as we did not want to make it public—the three of us, Mr Smith, Mr Walker and myself, went to the place and made a small hole, just enough to admit a man's head and shoulders. The doorway opened into a passage, and round the corner to the left was the vault proper. We all scrambled in, and by the light of a candle which we carried, we saw two chests lying side by side. I cannot say how many chests there were. There would be half a dozen as far as I can

St Rule's Tower

The Haunted Tower

remember. I saw the body of a girl. The
body was stiff and mummified-like.
What appeared to be a glove was on
one of the hands...After we went in the
first time we shut up the hole and kept
the matter a profound secret, and I did
not know that anyone knew of it except
ourselves. People had been in the habit
of calling the place the Haunted Tower
and when going to the harbour they
ran past it. No one had any idea that it
was a place of burial till we opened it.'

When Linskill himself reopened the Tower at midnight on the 21st August 1888, he found nothing
more than scattered bits of coffins and a few skel-
etons. He was similarly unsuccessful in his search
for the secret passages which he believed existed in

the vicinity of the cathedral.

> 'It is a sad, nay, a melancholy fact (for I
> have been told this by the very best
> authorities) that *I am not psychic*,
> despite the fact that I have spent days
> and nights in gloomy, grimly-haunted
> chambers and ruins, and even a
> lonesome Hallowe'en night on the
> summit of St Rule's ancient tower (my
> only companions being sandwiches,
> matches, some cigars, and the
> necessary and indispensable flask), yet,
> alas! I have *never* heard or seen
> anything the least abnormal, or felt the
> necessary, or much talked of, mystic
> presence.'
>
> **W. T. Linskill**
> *St Andrews Ghost Stories* (1921)

Close to the tower is one of the most interesting
stones in the graveyard, which depicts a 19th century ship under full sail. On closer inspection the
stone tells the tragic story of one family's atrocious
ill fortune. The stone was erected in 1836 by Esther
and William Wallace, in memory of their four sons—
three of whom were drowned: John Wallace,
drowned in the Thames in 1803, aged 16; Thomas
Wallace, drowned in the Amazon in 1815, aged 21;
and William Wallace, Commander of the Brig *Rival*,
'perished with all on board on the coast of Ireland'
in 1832, aged 39. Just to the north of St Rule's Tower
are two other interesting stones. One is that of:

CARL GOTTFRIED FERDINAND TIEGS,
BORN 15TH SEPR 1810 IN HENKENHAGEN
BY COLBERG IN PRUSSIA. DIED IN THE

BAY OF ST ANDREWS 21ST OCTOBER 1839,
ON BOARD OF THE GALLIOT DELPHIN OF COLBERG.

and the other is that of:

MR DAVID DUNLOP A NATIVE OF PAISLEY AND
FOUNDATION BURSAR OF THE UNITED COLLEGE
ST ANDREWS WHO PERISHED WHEN BATHING
IN THE WITCH LAKE 22ND JULY 1812 AGED 19
YEARS. ERECTED IN TESTIMONY OF THEIR
ESTEEM AND AFFECTION BY HIS PROFESSORS
AND FELLOW STUDENTS

From here, walk back past the north side of the cathedral ruins, leave the cathedral precinct by the North Transept gate and turn right onto the path to the harbour.

To the north east of the cathedral are the fragmentary cliff-top ruins of the 12th century Culdee church of **St Mary of the Rock**. The Culdees were the first Christians to come to St Andrews—St Mary of the Rock may have been established as early as the 9th century—but by the 12th century their function as keepers of the shrine of St Andrew had passed to the **Augustinian Order**, and the position of their church outside the walls of the cathedral symbolised their gradual exclusion from its work. This exclusion, which resulted from the apparent incompatibility of the secular Culdees and the (theoretically) more spiritual canons regular, was probably complete by the middle of the 13th century. The Culdees were, however, given the opportunity of becoming canons regular, but few took up this offer, and they stuck it out on their cliff top in the face of prolonged Papal, Royal, and Augustinian disapproval. Their numbers gradually dwindled, and little is known of what became of them after the 14th century. The

The Long Pier

Church of the Rock was destroyed in 1559 during the Reformation.

Walk down the path to the left and you will come to the start of the Long Pier.

The Long Pier, which replaced a wooden one destroyed in a storm in 1655, dates from the 17th century and was constructed using stone taken from the castle.

*Continue along Shorehead until you come to the Sea Yett, the medieval eastern gateway to the town which leads onto **The Pends**. At the top of The Pends is the structure from which this road derives its name, 'pend' meaning a passage through a building. Just before you reach the top of The Pends, you will see a lane leading off to the left. This is known as Nun's Walk and leads to **St Leonard's Chapel**.*

This was originally the chapel of St Leonard's College, which was founded here in 1512 by **Archbishop Alexander Stewart** and **Prior John Hepburn**. The College was built on the site of an earlier Hospital of St Leonard, which had served the pilgrims to the shrine of St Andrew. The buildings arranged around the central courtyard now form part of St Leonard's School. The chapel itself fell into disrepair in the middle of the 18th century when the College was amalgamated with St Salvator's, and it remained roofless until 1910.

The Pends was the original entrance to the Cathedral Precinct, and what remains is the roofless 14th century vaulted gatehouse. The corbels which supported the roof are still visible. The Pends was originally reserved for the sole use of the cathedral, and it was not opened as a public road until the 19th century.

From The Pends turn right and you are back outside Deans Court; or you may wish to go straight onto Walk 4—South Street and St Mary's at this point.

3

THE UNIVERSITY WALK

All Saints Episcopal Church
Younger Hall
St Salvators
Old Union
Library
Crawford Centre
Greyfriars Gardens

Starting Point: All Saints Episcopal Church
in North Castle St

Recommended Map
St Andrews Street Plan (4th Edition)

Distance: 1 mile

Tearooms
Brambles, College St
Old Union, North St
Ladyhead Coffee Shop, North St

St Andrews University was founded on 28th February 1412 when its Charter was drawn up by **Bishop Henry Wardlaw** in the Chapter House of the cathedral. This Charter was intended to formalise the teaching that had been going on in St Andrews since 1410. The university could not, however, confer degrees on its students; that could only be done once Papal approval had been granted. This presented something of a problem because, as often happened in the middle ages, there was some dispute as to who was currently the true Pope. It was eventually decided that an application should be made to **Antipope Benedict XIII** who was based in Aragon. On 28 August 1413 Benedict issued the required Papal Bulls which meant that the university could now teach and present degrees in theology, canon and civil law, arts, medicine and 'other lawful faculties'. The Papal Bulls were brought back to Scotland by Henry Ogilvy on the 3rd February 1414 amid scenes of great rejoicing.

At this stage the university did not have a Principal; instead the Rector performed that function, and the first Rector was **Laurence of Lindores,** an *'Inquisitor of Heretical Pravity'*. It is worth noting that the university did not even own any property until 1419, when a small tenement in South Street, on the site of the present South Street library, was donated.

The original Colleges of the university were **St Salvator's** (1450), **St Leonard's** (1512), **Blackfriars** (1516), and **St Mary's** (1538), their main purpose being the education of the clergy. Blackfriars only survived until the late 1550's, and the decline in student numbers in the 18th century—**Daniel Defoe** commented on the sad state St Salvator's had fallen into by the first decade of the 18th century—led to

St Salvator's and St Leonard's combining to form **The United College** in 1747. St Mary's became the Faculty of Divinity at the end of the 19th century. Dr Johnson also commented on the decline of the university in the 1770's:

> 'But whoever surveys the world must
> see many things that give him pain.
> The kindness of the professors did not
> contribute to abate the uneasy
> remembrance of a university declining,
> a College alienated, and a Church
> profaned and hastening to the ground.
> The distance of a calamity from the
> present time seems to preclude the
> mind from contact of sympathy. Events
> long past are barely known: they are
> not considered. We read with as little
> emotion the violence of Knox and his
> followers, as the irruptions of Alaric
> and the Goths. Had the university been
> destroyed two centuries ago, we
> should not have regretted it; but to see
> it pining in decay and struggling for
> life, fills the mind with mournful
> images and ineffectual wishes.'
> **Dr Samuel Johnson**
> *Journey to the Western Islands* (1773)

The walk begins at All Saints Episcopal Church in North Castle Street.

All Saints Episcopal Church (1) in North Castle Street is situated within a charming small courtyard. Most of the buildings are not of any great age—everything dates from the first quarter of the 20th century, apart from the house on the north side of the courtyard which is 17th century.

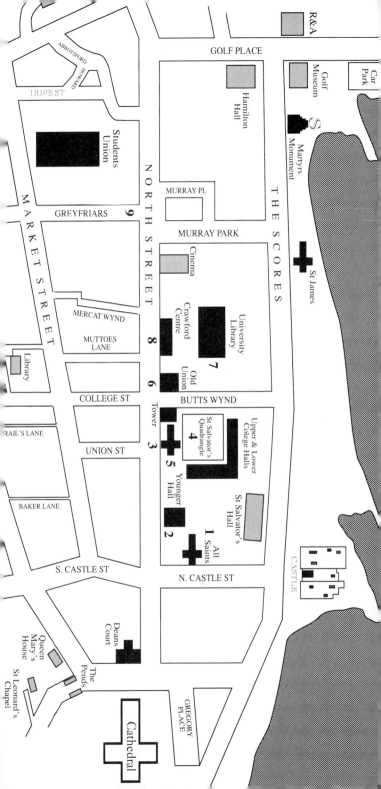

Go straight across the courtyard and into the church—the door is just to the left inside the colonnaded walkway. Once inside if you turn right you will see a fine model of a sailing ship suspended from the roof. The only other interesting feature inside the church is the extremely elaborate, though again not very old, wooden font cover. Shaped like a medieval spire, this curious object is suspended on a pulley and swings to and fro if touched.

*Leaving All Saints, turn right up North Castle St to North St. Just to the left (across the road) is the St Andrews Preservation Trust Museum, which has a variety of exhibits in a beautifully restored building. Head west along North St, passing the unremarkable modern addition to St Salvator's Hall of residence, **Gannochy House**, on your right. The next major building on the right is the **Younger Hall (2)**.*

The Younger Hall was built between 1923 and 1929 and is a vast, imposing and rather crude addition to North Street. Designed in a pseudo-classical style, the building's appearance is not enhanced by the confused temple motifs—urns, torches and columns—that make up its northern facade. The Hall itself now serves as the setting for the university's graduation ceremonies and matriculation rituals.

*Continue along North Street to **St Salvator's College (3)**, Chapel and Quadrangle, just beyond the university offices and directly opposite Martyrs Church.*

St Salvators was founded in August 1450 by **Bishop James Kennedy,** and it combined a college for the study of theology and the arts with a collegiate church. The massive 125 foot tower dates from the 1460's, although the spire was a later addition by

Archbishop John Hamilton in 1550. The parapet and the clock are both mid-Victorian additions. To the right of the Tower is the Chapel, with the remains of a small cemetery in front of it.

Before going through the archway under the Tower and into the quadrangle, take note of the letters 'PH' set into the cobbles in front of the Tower. These are the initials of **Patrick Hamilton** (1504-1528), the first martyr of the Scottish Reformation, who was burned at the stake on this spot on 29th February 1528. It is considered bad luck for undergraduates to step on the letters PH on their way to exams . . .

Hamilton was a young aristocrat who had studied at Paris and Louvain and had been influenced by Luther. On his return to St Andrews, he began to preach these heretical reformed doctrines. He was soon arrested, tried in the cathedral, and condemned to be burnt at the stake. His executioners, however, were incompetent and the fire kept going out, with the result that Hamilton was still alive and unrepentant after six hours. Some thought that this was the end of Protestantism in St Andrews, but a more accurate assessment was provided by of one of Cardinal James Beaton's associates who told him:

> 'if ye will burn them, let them be burnt
> in deep cellars, for the reek of Master
> Patrick Hamilton has infected as many
> as it blew upon.'

At the front of St Salvator's Tower, just above the coat of arms of Bishop Kennedy, you will notice what appears to be a crude carving of a man's face on one of the stones. This is said to be the face of Patrick Hamilton, supernaturally etched onto the stone at the time of his execution.

*Go through the archway and into the **Quadrangle** (4), passing the Hebdomadars building and Porters lodge on the left.*

The quadrangle was completely rebuilt in the first half of the 19th century by **Robert Reid**, who was responsible for the east side; and **William Nixon** who constructed the north side, including **Lower College Hall**, in 1845-6. These buildings replaced the original cloister court which had stood here till the second half of the 18th century.

Reminiscent of Oxbridge colleges, the 'Quad,' as it is known to students, is the site of the anarchic festivities that take place annually on **'Raisin Monday'**. During the course of this long established event, students dressed in outlandish costumes throw all manner of noxious substances—rotten eggs, anchovies, shaving foam, and vast quantities of flour and water—at each other and generally create havoc. This is all done in the cause of initiating the more junior members of the university into the arcane and unusual traditions of the place. The annual Graduation Ball is held in a marquee on the lawns to the north of **Lower College Hall**.

After going around the Quad, go into the Chapel by the door in the cloister to the east of the tower.

St Salvator's Chapel (5) was built between 1450 and 1460. From the 1560's it was used as a court, before being restored to its original function in the 1760's. The cloister you pass through before entering the chapel dates from the mid-Victorian restora-

St Salvator's Quad

tion of the quadrangle. Passing through the ancient wooden door, you enter the ante-chapel, above which is the organ loft.

At the west end of the chapel there are a number of memorials; one commemorates **Major John Cook VC**, and another is that of **Lt William Dalgleish Playfair** of the Bengal Native Infantry, who was killed in 1846 aged 25:

> 'His mortal remains lie near the field
> of battle, in a soldiers grave, unmarked
> and now unknown.'

Moving on into the main body of the chapel you will see the elaborate oak stalls which date from the early 20th century, and, to the right of the communion table, the pulpit. This pulpit was transferred here from **Holy Trinity Church** in the 1930's and is believed to be the same one that was used by **John Knox** in the 16th century.

> 'In the opening upe of his text he was moderat the space of an hallf houre; bot when he enterit to application, he maid me sa to shudder and tremble, that I could nocht hald a pen to wryt.'
> **James Melville**
> *A 16th century St Andrews student, describing one of Knox's sermons*

At the east end of the chapel, behind the communion table, there is a war memorial, and in a niche to the left is the tomb of the college's founder, **Bishop James Kennedy** who died in 1465.

This tomb, with its black marble slab and French carving, apparently designed by Kennedy himself, was originally much more ornate, but it was severely damaged in 1773. The university authorities had decided that they did not care for the echo that the old stone-vaulted roof gave the chapel, so, after seeking the advice of **James Craig** (the youthful designer of Edinburgh's New Town), they demolished the roof, with disastrous results for the interior of the chapel and the founder's tomb. Craig then provided them with the present wooden roof. The tomb itself was partially restored in the 1930's.

> *Leave the chapel by the same door and head back out through the archway onto North Street. Turn right and just across Butts Wynd is the* **Old Union (6)**.

The Old Union probably dates from the 15th century, although its present facade was remodelled in the 18th century. In 1891 what had until then been a private house was bought and converted into a students union thanks to a donation from the 3rd Marquis of Bute, who also restored Falkland Palace in the 1890's. The Old Union building is traditionally thought to have been the house of the **'Admirable Crichton'**, who was a student at St Andrews from 1569-74.

James Crichton of Eliock (1560-1582) was the son of the Lord Advocate and he came to St Andrews aged only nine. After graduating five years later, he became something of an international celebrity as a result of his public speaking exploits in Italy. By the time he was 20 he had mastered at least ten languages, and could speak with complete authority on virtually any subject. Crichton was also an excellent gymnast, horseman and swordsman, but his remarkable life was to end in tragedy. In 1582, whilst in the service of the Duke of Mantua, he was stabbed to death in the street. He was only 21.

Inside the Old Union there is a small coffee shop, one section of which still retains its original vaulting. On one of the beams there is a list of former Rectors of the university, including **J. M. Barrie** and **John Cleese**.

*Continuing along North Street, the **University Library (7)** is on the right just before the Crawford Centre. **The Crawford Centre (8)**, at 93 North Street, is an arts centre that hosts a variety of exhibitions throughout the year. During term time its theatre is also the venue for the university drama society's productions. From the Crawford Centre, walk down North Street until you reach **Greyfriars Gardens (9)** on the left.*

Greyfriars Gardens was built in the 1830's as part of a scheme to link the three main streets of the town. But the name Greyfriars comes from the old Franciscan friary that was established here by Bishop Kennedy in 1458. In the 1470's the Franciscans in St Andrews had the support of James IV; but less than 100 years later their house was completely destroyed by the reformers in 1559. Greyfriars featured in a particularly unlikely ghost story recounted by **Dean Linskill** in his book *St Andrews Ghost Stories*. He claimed that one of his friends was haunted by the skull of a medieval monk who was murdered in the monastery chapel.

> 'He has tried every means possible to
> get rid of that monk's skull; but they
> are of no avail, it always returns. So he
> has made the best he can of it, and
> keeps it in a locked casket in an empty
> room at the end of a wing of the old
> house. He says it keeps fairly quiet, but
> on stormy nights wails and gruesome
> shrieks are heard from the casket in
> that closed apartment. I heard from
> him last week. He said: "Dear W.T.L., I
> don't think I mentioned that twice a
> year the skull of Neville de Beauchamp
> vanishes from its casket for a period of
> about two days. It is never away
> longer. I wonder if it still haunts its old
> monastery at St Andrews where its
> owner was slain. Do write and tell me
> if anyone now in that vicinity hears or
> sees the screaming skull of my
> ancestor, Neville de Beauchamp." '

Walk along Greyfriars Gardens to the junction with Bell Street and Market Street. Turn right and you will see the modern students union building on the right. This marks the end of the walk.

4

SOUTH STREET AND ST MARY'S

Queen Mary's House
St Marys
West Gardens
Holy Trinity Church
Blackfriars Chapel
Madras College
Loudens Close
West Port

Starting Point: The Pends
at the end of South St

Opening Times
Queen Mary's House open by appointment only.
(Contact St Leonards School on 0334 78102.)
Holy Trinity Church open at various times, or
contact Rev Charles Armour (0334 74494) for
further details.

Recommended Map
St Andrews Street Plan (4th edition)

Distance: 1 mile

Tearooms
Merchants House, 49 South Street

*From **The Pends (1)** turn left into South Street. Immediately to the left is the building traditionally known as **Queen Mary's House (2)**.*

The house takes its name from the period when it was used by **Mary Queen of Scots** in 1564. The East wing of the house was sold in the 18th century and was rebuilt as Priorsgate. Queen Mary's House itself dates from the 1520's and was built by **Hugh Scrymgeour**, a local merchant. Several additions were made in the 17th and 18th centuries, before the house was converted into a library for St Leonard's School by **Reginald Fairlie** in the 1920's.

On the opposite side of the street is the house known as **The Roundel** as a result of its fine balustraded tower. This house dates from the 16th century, but the balustrade was one of a number of 17th century additions.

Continue along South Street, past the junction of Abbey Street and South Castle Street, and then past West Burn Lane until you reach the entrance to St Mary's College (3) on the left.

St Mary's College was founded in 1538 by **Archbishop James Beaton** with the aim of combating the spread of heresy by creating a better educated clergy. The college was not completed until the time of **Archbishop Hamilton** almost 20 years later, although much of the work seems to have been done by French masons in the first five years after the college's founding. The western range of the college is all that remains today, and much of this part was rebuilt in the 1620's and the 1820's, while retaining some of the original features and character of the earlier work.

The most celebrated Principal of St Mary's was **Andrew Melville** (1545-1622) who attended St Mary's before going to study at Paris, Poitiers and Geneva. By 1578 Melville had become Moderator of the General Assembly, in 1579 he began the reorganisation of St Andrews University, and in 1580 he became Principal of St Mary's.

Ironically, Melville intended the main function of the university to be the promotion of reformed theology to combat the Catholic propagandists of the Counter-Reformation. This was more or less the exact opposite of what James Beaton had intended when he established St Mary's in 1538. Melville worked tirelessly for the cause of Presbyterianism, and his fanaticism brought him into conflict with the Crown—with the result that he was a prisoner in the Tower of London from 1605-11. He was released but forced to go into exile and was never able to return to Scotland. He died at Sedan in1622.

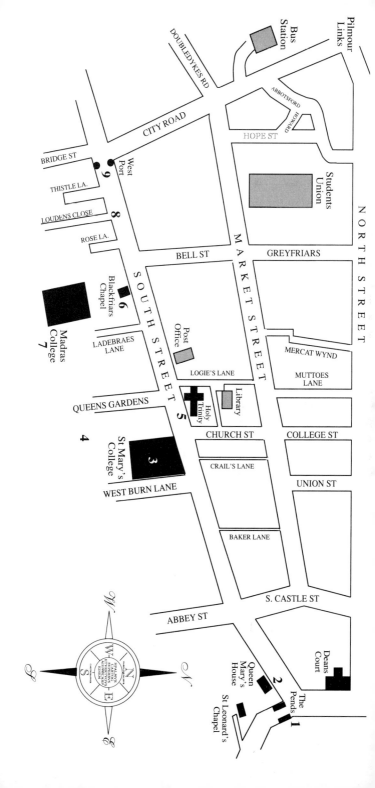

St Mary's College today is one of the finest parts of the modern university, its ancient buildings combining well with the beautiful setting of trees, lawns and gardens. Passing through the entrance gateway with its inscription *'In Principio Erat Verbum'*, you will see the enormous Holm Oak tree directly ahead. This tree has been here since the middle of the 18th century and is still flourishing, despite some of its branches needing a little artificial help to stay aloft. The main building on the right houses the **Divinity Department**, the entrance to which is through the low doorway in the crowstep tower.

One of the department's lecture halls still retains the sort of old-fashioned, and decidedly uncomfortable, wooden benches of which Andrew Melville would undoubtedly have approved.

One of the phases of the college's rebuilding is commemorated by a plaque on the wall of the main building, 'R.M.H. 1621'—the initials being those the Principal of the time, Robert Howie. Just to the right of the tower is a thorn tree, a 1940's replacement for one reputed to have been planted by **Mary Queen of Scots** in the 1560's. Close to the tree is a sundial which was placed here by Professor Comrie in 1664. The rather solitary, overgrown gateway on the lawn to the left dates from the 17th century, but it has only stood in its present position since the beginning of this century.

Before leaving St Mary's, walk down the path to the right of the sundial and continue along it until you reach the entrance to the **West Garden (4)**. This is an excellent place to pause, take advantage of the benches, and absorb the tranquillity of the place.

St Mary's

*Leaving St Mary's go back onto South Street and turn left, continuing along to **Holy Trinity Church (5)**, which is on the right, opposite Queens Gardens and the Tourist Information Centre.*

Holy Trinity Church was the name of the town parish church from the middle of the 12th century, when the first church of that name was built within the precinct of the cathedral. This earlier church stood a little to the east of the cathedral and was used from the 12th century to the 15th century, when the South Street Church replaced it. The old church disappeared when the Hepburns dismantled it for use in the rebuilding of the precinct wall. The church that now stands in South Street was begun in 1410, but little remains of that building other than the tower, as the church was extensively altered at the end of the 18th century and then completely rebuilt by P. MacGregor Chambers between 1907 and 1909. This later work was intended to restore the church to its medieval splendour and employed so many different medieval devices—the east window, for example, is said to be a scaled down version of Carlisle Cathedral's unique east window—that it has been called 'a dictionary of architectural quotations'.

Holy Trinity Church is probably best known for its association with **John Knox**, who first preached here in 1547 and who later used the church as his platform for the sermon that led to the looting of the cathedral, and the destruction of much else, in the name of Reformation in June 1559. When he visited St Andrews in 1773, **Dr Johnson** held Knox responsible for much of the ecclesiastical decay he saw around him. When he overheard someone ask where Knox was buried he answered "I hope in the highway; I have been looking at his deformations."

John Knox (c.1514-1572) was born either at Haddington or at Morham in East Lothian and was educated at St Andrews University, although he did not take a degree. He studied scripture and the teachings of St Augustine, but it was only when he came under the influence of **George Wishart** (who was later burned at the stake for heresy by Cardinal Beaton—*see Walk 1, The Castle*) that he became involved with the work of the reformers. After the execution of Wishart in 1546, Knox joined the Castilians in the defence of St Andrews Castle against the Regent Arran and the French fleet of the Prior of Capua. Once the castle fell, Knox became a prisoner in the French galleys until his release two years later. After that he became a Royal Chaplain at the court of **Edward VI**, before the accession of **Mary Tudor** (1516-58) forced him to go abroad. In Switzerland he was much influenced by the teachings of **John Calvin**, and he returned to Scotland in 1559 to become the major figure in the Scottish Reformation.

By 1559 the reformers were gaining influential support, as was seen in the formation of the **'Lords of the Congregation'**—powerful members of the nobility who swore to support the reformers. Beginning with his sermon at Perth on 11th May 1559, Knox travelled through Scotland denouncing the corruption of the medieval church and organising the casting down of its images and the destruction of its property. These disturbances reached St Andrews in early June with the attacks on Holy Trinity, Blackfriars, Greyfriars, St Mary's of the Rock and the cathedral itself.

By the end of August 1560, the **Reformation Parliament** had formally ended the authority of the Pope in Scotland and the new Kirk adopted the **Book of Common Order**, which was much the same as that used by Knox when he had been a minister in Calvin's Geneva.

Knox spent the rest of his life struggling to uphold the work of reformation, but he also found time to write his own *'History of the Reformation'*, before he died in 1572. The pulpit Knox is believed to have preached from in Holy Trinity in June 1559 was moved to St Salvator's Chapel in the 1930's and can still be seen there today.

Inside Holy Trinity Church the most interesting feature is the black and white marble memorial to the murdered **Archbishop James Sharp** in the South Transept. This was made by Dutch Craftsmen in the 1680's and brought to St Andrews by Sharp's son, William Sharp of Scotscraig. Archbishop Sharp was killed by a group of Covenanters as he rode in his coach across Magus Muir near St Andrews on May 3rd 1679. *(See Magus Muir—Walk 8.)*

> *Leaving Holy Trinity Church, turn right and continue along to the ruins of **Blackfriars Chapel** (6) on the left, in front of Madras College.*

Blackfriars Chapel is the ruined fragment of the north transept of the 16th century church of the Dominican Order in St Andrews. The Dominicans were probably brought to St Andrews by **Bishop Malvoisine** in the 13th century and their house was established in South Street in the 1270's. The house and the church were destroyed during the Reformation. It is possible that Cardinal David Beaton may have been buried here in 1547 after his body was recovered from the bottle dungeon of the castle. Directly behind Blackfriars Chapel is **Madras College (7)**.

Madras College was designed by **William Burn** and opened in 1833. Its founder was the **Rev Dr Andrew Bell** (1753-1832) who was born in the town and studied at the university before going to India. He became chaplain to the **East India Company** and invented a system of elementary education known as the Madras System while in charge of the military orphanage in Madras. Returning to Britain towards the end of the 18th century, Bell concentrated on promoting his system—which involved the older pupils in the education of their juniors. At the end of his life he donated £50,000 to be used to establish a school based on his system in his home town. The result was this Jacobean style building, with its elegant curvilinear gables and fine bay windows.

*Continue along the street, past the junction with Bell Street to **Louden's Close (8)**.*

Loudens Close (146 South Street) is a good example of a medieval close. The house that faced onto the street would originally have backed onto a strip of land serving as a smallholding for the occupants. Strips of land such as this were known as **'rigs'**. As time went on this land would usually be built upon, the close being formed by these new houses built at right angles to the main street. A small entrance to the close from the street would then have to be made in the original house, with the resulting passage generally being named after the owner. Louden's Close displays all the signs of just such a development, although it owes at least some of its present appearance to the restoration work carried out in 1939-49 by **J. C. Cunningham** for the St Andrews Preservation Trust.

Right at the end of South Street is **The West Port (9)**—built in 1589 on the site of an earlier gate and modelled on the Netherbow Port in Edinburgh—and this marks the end of the walk.

This walk can be extended by going straight on to the Lade Braes Walk which starts at Louden's Close.

5

LADE BRAES

Loudens Close
Lade Braes Walk
Park
Law Mill
Botanic Garden

Starting Point: **Loudens Close**
at the west end of South Street,
near the National Trust Shop

Opening Times
Botanic Garden: summer 10am-7pm,
For winter opening, check with the tourist
information office (0334 72021). Entry 50p.

Recommended Maps
St Andrews Street Plan (4th Edition)

Distance: One and a half miles

Loudens Close (1) at 146 South Street is a good example of a medieval close. The house that faced onto the street would originally have backed onto a strip of land serving as a smallholding for the occupants of the house. Strips of land such as this were known as **'rigs'**. As time went by this land would usually be built upon, and the close would be formed with these new houses being built at right angles to the main street. A small entrance to the close from the street would then have to be made in the original house, with the resulting passage generally being named after the owner. Loudens Close displays all the signs of just such a development, although it owes at least some of its present appearance to the restoration work carried out in 1939-49 by **J. C. Cunningham**.

Walk through Loudens Close and down the narrow lane until it joins Lade Braes. Turn right and walk along Lade Braes to the point where it crosses Bridge Street.

Lade Braes originally formed the southern boundary of the town, until more housing was built in this area in the late 19th century. The walls that run along Lade Braes west of Loudens Close were part of the defences of the town. Although the town was never completely walled, the defences around the cathedral precinct and the walls and dykes that ran behind the main streets formed quite an effective series of defences. The only way into the town was through the town gates, such as the **Sea Yett** at the bottom of The Pends, or the **West Port** (built in 1589 on the site of an earlier gate and modelled on the Netherbow Port in Edinburgh) at the west end of South Street.

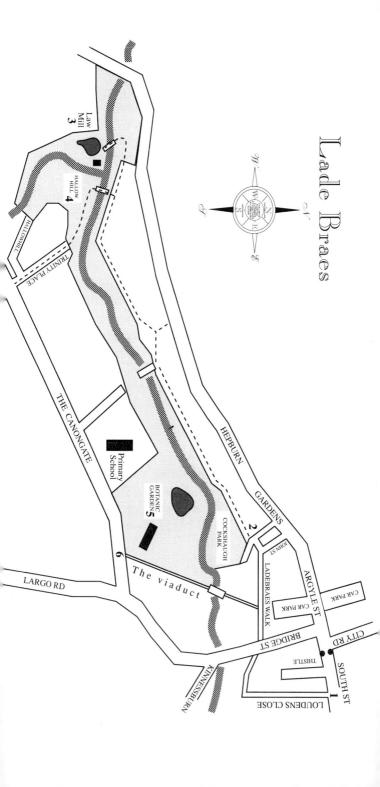

*Cross Bridge Street at Melbourne Place and continue along Lade Braes to **Cockshaugh Park (2)**.*

After passing the main playing field, either take the lower path that runs alongside the **Kinness Burn** (where you can take a break on one of the benches and feed the ducks), or follow the higher path that runs above it. Continue along here until you reach the ruins of **Law Mill (3)** with its duckpond.

From here go back across the bridge below the pond, turn right and walk along to the next bridge. Cross this bridge and head up **Hallow Hill (4)** to **Trinity Place** which leads onto **The Canongate**. Turn left and walk past the primary school to the **University Botanic Garden (5)**. Although not particularly large, the Botanic Garden has a wide variety of plants and trees and a stepped ornamental pond with lilies and reeds. There are also a number of glasshouses.

From the Botanic Garden go back onto The Canongate and continue along until you come to the **Viaduct Walk (6)** on your left. This walkway leads back across the Kinness Burn to Lade Braes Walk. Turn right, cross Bridge Street, and return to Loudens Close.

6

THE OLD COURSE

The Royal & Ancient
First Tee
Old Bridge
Swilken Burn
Famous Holes & Bunkers
The British Golf Museum

Starting Point: Royal & Ancient Golf Club
on Golf Place off North Street

Opening Times
Sunday is the only day of the week when it is
possible to walk here, as no golf is played on the
Old Course on the Sabbath

Recommended Map
St Andrews Street Plan (4th edition)

Tearooms
The Scores Hotel
Rusacks Marine Hotel, Pilmour Links

*'Golf is a game where the ball invariably lies badly
and the golfer well'*
G. F. Stout

The Royal & Ancient

The game of golf originated at least as far back as the mid 15th century, when it began to replace archery as the most popular sport of the common people. Things got so bad that **James II** was forced to forbid the playing of golf, as archery practise was beginning to suffer. Royal approval came when **James IV** took up the game, and **Mary Queen of Scots** became the first woman player in the 16th century. By the start of the 17th century the game was being played using wooden balls, and one of St Andrews most celebrated students, **James Graham, 1st Marquis of Montrose**, played while he was at the university in the late 1620's.

The game didn't really take off until the formation of **The Society of St Andrews Golfers** in 1754. A group of local gentry and nobility formed themselves into a society to take part in 'the Anticient and healthfull exercise of the Golf' and to play in an annual competition for a silver golf club. The winner of the Silver Club also became the **'Captain of the Golf'** for the following year. This contest replaced the annual archery contest, during which students of the university competed for a silver arrow. From 1824 the Captain of the club was decided by the members rather than by competition, each new Captain teeing off from the first at 8am on the day of the club's AGM.

The first winner of the Silver Club was **William Landale**, a merchant, although his score is not recorded. **William St Clair** of Roslin managed a score of 121 in 1764; but this was for 22 holes. The finest performance of the 18th century was that of **James Durham** of Largo House who took only 94 strokes to complete 18 holes in 1767, a score that was not beaten until the middle of the 19th century. Scores began to improve dramatically as the design of golf clubs and balls progressed. The wooden ball had quickly been replaced by a device known as the **Old Feathery**, which was a leather ball stuffed with feathers. The Old Feathery was, however, quite difficult to make and fairly expensive; added to which it rarely lasted more than one round. The longest drive with one of these balls was 361 yards, achieved by Samuel Messieux at the start of the 19th century.

The Old Feathery was replaced by the **Guttie**, invented by the Paterson family of St Andrews in 1845. This revolutionary new ball was made of Gutta Percha, a rubbery substance, some of which had been sent from Malaya to Paterson Senior, and the experiments of his two sons on the Old Course

Old Tom Morris

led to the marketing of the Guttie in 1846. The main advantages of the Guttie were that it was cheaper and lasted longer than the Old Feathery. The Guttie remained the standard ball until it was replaced by the modern golf ball at the turn of the century. This ball, unlike its predecessors, was not a St Andrews invention—it originated in America.

From 1834, when **William IV** became the club's patron, the Society of St Andrews Golfers became the **Royal and Ancient**. The present clubhouse was built in 1854, and soon afterwards the first Open Championship was held. By the end of the 19th century the R&A was the accepted ruling body of the game.

The development of the **Old Course** in the second half of the 19th century owed much to the influence of the celebrated golfer **Old Tom Morris**. Old Tom was one of the best known golfers of the 19th century, along with other characters like **Allan Robertson** (who once took just 95 strokes to complete a round of the Old Course using only a driver), but his main influence was as R&A greenkeeper and professional from 1865. Old Tom won the Open four times, and his son **Young Tom Morris** was to win the Open in 1870, 1871 and 1872, before dying in 1875 aged only 24.

The Old Course itself is usually around 6,500 yards long; although it is lengthened to nearer 7,000 during the Open Championship. The curious names of its bunkers, fairways and holes, and the stories associated with them, are legendary—from the **Valley of Sin** to **The Principal's Nose**.

One of the best anecdotes of the Old Course is the

story of **Captain Maitland Dougall's** round, played in October 1860. When he was just about to tee off, he heard that a ship was in trouble in St Andrews Bay. The weather was so bad, however, that nobody was keen to join the lifeboat crew. Maitland Dougall, however, did not hesitate to take his place in the boat, as James Balfour wrote in his book *Reminiscences of Golf on St Andrews Links* (1887):

> 'The men were rescued, and the lifeboat came ashore in the afternoon. The play for the medal was begun after the arrival of the lifeboat. The wind was still furious. It was to Maitland Dougall's credit that, though his arms were sore, and he was stiff and all wet, he gained the Club gold medal at 112 strokes.'

One of the most famous bunkers is **Hell bunker**, of which the following, no doubt apocryphal, tale is often told. A certain Bishop found his drive had gone astray and landed in Hell bunker, but he managed to play a fine stroke to extricate himself from its depths. Seeing his miraculous escape, his caddie observed: 'Mind noo when ye die tae tak yer niblick wi ye'.

The British Golf Museum, opposite the Royal & Ancient Clubhouse, has a huge variety of exhibits and information about the history and development of golf—from the earliest reference to golf in a Statute of 1457 to the earliest surviving rules, thirteen in total, dating from 1744 (there are thirty four in the modern game). It seems almost impossible that anyone could have put together a round of golf with some of the early clubs and golf balls, but even with the feather ball, drives of around 200 yards were possible in the 1840's. The game was relatively expensive for many centuries, and in the late 17th century a ball cost 4 shillings, a wooden club 12 shillings and an iron club 24 shillings. As the equipment became less expensive and more refined during the 19th century, more and more people took up the game. The Museum has excellent displays including hi-tech touch sensitive screens which tell the stories behind the Open Championship and include details of the lives of famous golfers from Old Tom Morris to the present day. There are also displays of clubs donated by golfers including Nick Faldo, Gary Player and Jack Nicklaus. And you can even play a round of the Old Course on the video game—nearly as difficult as the real thing!

It is possible to walk around the Old Course on Sundays when no play takes place.

7

EAST SANDS TO KINGSBARNS

Shorehead
Harbour
Beach
Leisure Centre
Cliffs
Kinkell Braes
The Rock & Spindle
Buddo Ness
Pitmilly Burn
Kingsbarns

Starting Point: **The Harbour**

Opening Times
For the East Sands Leisure Centre,
0334 76506

Recommended Maps
Ordnance Survey Landranger 59
St Andrews Street Plan (4th Edition)

Distance: 7 miles

Tearooms
Merchants House, South Street,
Ladyhead Coffee Shop

Cross the harbour by the narrow footbridge at
Shorehead and continue straight onto the beach.

Shorehead was redeveloped in the mid 1960's and most of the buildings that stood here were demolished. It had been the place where many of the local fishermen lived, until it was declared a slum in 1935. One of the tenements that lined the harbour was known as *The Royal George* —the name coming from a ship of the line.

The harbour itself was largely rebuilt in the mid 19th century, although the long pier, which replaced a wooden one destroyed in a storm in 1655, dates from the 17th century and was constructed using stone taken from the castle. This pier nowadays regularly serves as the backdrop to another unusual university tradition, **The Pier Walk**, during which students dressed in red gowns walk down to the pier from St Salvators Chapel in North Street, along to the end of the pier and then back to town. The walk apparently originated as a memorial to a Divinity student, **John Honey**, who rescued seven men shipwrecked in the East Bay in 1800.

Walk along the East Sands and on your right you
will pass the new leisure centre which opened in
April 1988 and includes a Mediterranean style
swimming pool plus all the usual sports facilities.
At the end of the beach follow the path up the cliffs
onto the coastal walk.

Coastal Walk to Kingsbarns
(6 miles)

This path leads all the way round the coast to the beach at **Kingsbarns**. You will need a good pair of boots and remember to check the tides as the path is blocked at **Pitmilly Burn** at high tide.

The path passes the caravan park at **Kinkell Braes** and reaches the cliff top. From here there are excellent views back towards St Andrews and across to **Tentsmuir Forest**. A little further along you will see a large sandstone rock on the shore. This is known as **Maiden's Rock**.

From here the path descends to the shore and passes **Kinkell Cave**. This cave is situated in the cliffs and can only be reached from the shore at low tide.

Passing around **Kinkell Ness**, the path widens where it joins an old cart track. At one time there may have been a small harbour here. Continue along until you come to the **Rock and Spindle**. This is a volcanic rock formation and its name comes from its resemblance to a spinning wheel.

The path now runs quite close to the shore to **Buddo Ness**. On the way to Buddo Ness you will pass two Second World War pill boxes, and just after Buddo Ness is Buddo Rock, a large sandstone shore stack.

Continue along until you reach a low stone wall. A 19th century lifeboat station stood in the field close to this spot. From here follow the path either along the wall at the edge of the field, or on the shore to the slipway at the mouth of the **Pitmilly Burn**. At high tide, the burn can be avoided by following the burnside inland to the footbridge at Hillside farm. At low tide the path continues from the slipway on the other side of the burn to an old Salmon Bothy above a small sandy beach. The path follows the fence and then continues to **Babbet Ness**, before descending onto a long beach below the village of **Kingsbarns**. Here you can still see the remains of an old harbour, built in the traditional style of the East Neuk.

Close to the harbour is a car park, and the road leads from there up to the village of Kingsbarns with its old parish church—built in the 17th century and much altered at the start of the 19th century—and the 18th century village square, in the middle of which is a pump dated 1831.

8

MAGUS MUIR AND THE
SHARP MONUMENT

Magus Muir
Covenanters Graves
Sharp Monument
Woodland Walk

Starting Point: Signpost (1)

Directions to Start
Take the B939 west from St Andrews towards
Pitscottie. After about 2 miles turn left for Peat
Inn. 200 yards up this road there is a parking
space on the right and a signpost marking the
public footpath to the monument.

Recommended Map
Ordnance Survey Landranger 59

Distance: 1 mile

OS Map Reference: 459152

*The path leads through the wood for a few hundred yards before you come to the site of the **Covenanters Graves (2)**, marked by a stone surrounded by railings.*

This is the grave of a number of covenanters who were captured at the **Battle of Bothwell Brig** in the summer of 1679. Their execution here was an act of revenge for the murder of **Archbishop Sharp** earlier that same year. The inscription reads:

HERE LIES THOS BROWN JAMES WOOD ANDREW SWORD
JOHN WEDDELL & JOHN CLYDE WHO SUFFERED
MARTYRDOM ON MAGUS MUIR FOR THEIR ADHERENCE
TO THE WORD OF GOD AND SCOTLAND'S COVENANTED
WORK OF REFORMATION NOV 25 1679

CAUSE WE AT BOTHWELL DID APPEAR
PERJURIOUS OATHS REFUSED TO SWEAR
CAUSE WE CHRIST'S CAUSE WOULD NOT CONDEMN
WE WERE SENTENCED TO DEATH BY MEN
WHO RAGED AGAINST US IN SUCH FURY
OUR DEAD BODIES THEY DID NOT BURY
BUT UP ON POLES DID HING US HIGH
TRIUMPHS OF BABEL'S VICTORY
OUR LIVES WE FEARED NOT TO THE DEATH
BUT CONSTANT PRAYED TO OUR LAST BREATH

On the 22nd June 1679 the covenanting forces had been defending **Bothwell Bridge** on the road to Hamilton against the army of the **Duke of Monmouth**. When the covenanters ran out of ammunition, the Royalist forces easily overran them and many were captured and taken to Edinburgh, where they were held in terrible conditions in **Greyfriars Churchyard**. Those who survived either renounced their support for the **National Covenant**, or were transported to the colonies.

Returning to the main path, you will see the **Sharp Monument (3)**, a stone pyramid, on the right only a few yards further on, commemorating the murder of **Archbishop James Sharp** on 3rd May 1679. The inscription on the monument reads:

HUNC PROPE LOCUM JACOBUS SHARP
ARCHEPISCOPUS SANCTI ANDRAE A SALVIS
INIMICUS ADSTANTE FILIA SUA ET DEPRECANTE
TRUCICATIS EST AD MDCLXXIX

Archbishop James Sharp (1618-79) was born in Banff and educated at Aberdeen University, before becoming minister of Crail in 1648. Many of his colleagues felt he betrayed them when he accepted the Archbishopric of St Andrews in 1660.

He had gone to London to negotiate on behalf of his colleagues in the 'Resolutioner' faction, but changed sides and agreed to the restoration of the episcopacy in Scotland. Although he emerged as the Primate of Scotland, he had made many enemies in the process, who believed that he had sold out his religious principles in return for his Archbishopric. Sharp became even more unpopular when he gave his enthusiastic support to repressive measures being taken against the covenanters who absented themselves from church and took part in illegal conventicles.

It has been suggested that after the **Battle of Rullion Green** (1666), where **General Tam Dalyell** defeated a small and ill-equipped covenanting army in the Pentlands, Sharp suppressed a letter from the King that called for leniency for these amateur revolutionaries. Whether Sharp actually did this, or whether his enemies simply added it to the catalogue of his alleged misdeeds, many of those captured at Rullion Green were summarily executed and this episode did nothing to enhance his reputation.

One rumour that circulated at the time suggested that as a young man Sharp had fathered an illegitimate child, which he had subsequently strangled and buried under a hearthstone at the inn where he was staying. Years later, when he became Archbishop, the child's supposed mother repeatedly stood up in the Kirk and accused Sharp of this crime. Sharp had her silenced, and that seemed to be the end of the matter. However, when an old inn was being pulled down in Church Street in 1873, a child's skeleton was found under a hearthstone. As the repression of the covenanters reached its height in the 1670's—preaching at an outdoor conventicle

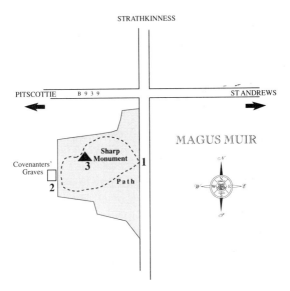

was a capital offence and vast fines were being exacted for non-attendance at church—Sharp became an obvious target for the anger of those on the receiving end.

Yet Sharp's murder on **Magus Muir** in May 1679 appears to have come about purely by chance. There was no conspiracy, and it was simple ill-fortune that led Sharp to meet a band of fanatical covenanters as he rode in his coach across the moor. These covenanters, including **Balfour of Kinloch** and **Hackston of Rathillet**, took full advantage of this chance meeting, dragged the Archbishop from his coach and shot and hacked him to death:

> 'The Bishop, when he saw them approach, called to his coachman to drive on; but the foremost horseman rode up to the window, shouting "Judas is taken!" and fired into the coach. The other seven came up. Hackston, with a curious casuistry staying apart, looked on during the threequarters of an hour which his comrades took to complete the slow murder of their victim....The commander then said, almost repeating the words of James Melvin when he slew Cardinal Beaton: "I take God to witness, whose cause I desire to own in adhering to this persecuted Gospel, that it is not out of hatred to thy person, nor for any prejudice thou hast done or could do to me, for which we intend to take thy life, but it is because thou hast been, and continues to be, an avowed opposer of the flourishing of Christ's kingdom, and murderer of His

saints, whose blood thou hast shed like water." Another of the band said to the Bishop, "Judas, repent"; to which he replied, "Save my life and I will save yours." His assailant rejoined, "It is neither in your power to save us nor to kill us"...The commander then fired his pistol, and one of his comrades wounded the Bishop with a shabble or pike. He at last came out of the coach, and while on his knees praying for life, was struck with two other wounds to the ground. More blows followed. His daughter cried from the coach, "This is murder!" to which she was answered, "Not murder, but God's vengeance on him for murdering many poor souls in the Kirk of Scotland." His footman called out he was dead; but one of the band, determined to make sure, alighted from his horse, and, thrusting his sword through the body till the blood spurted, said, "I am sure he is dead now."

J. G. Mackay
A History of Fife and Kinross (1895)

As the inscription on his tomb in Holy Trinity Church in St Andrews reads:

'despite his character and eminence nine sworn assassins, inspired by fanatical rage, did with pistols, swords and daggers most foully massacre close to his metropolitan seat, under the noonday sun, with his beloved eldest daughter and his personal attendants bleeding, weeping and protesting, on May 3rd 1679, in the sixty first year of his age, piercing him with countless

wounds when he had fallen on his
knees to pray even for his murderers.'

Only Hackston was eventually brought to justice. After fighting at the battles of **Drumclog** and **Bothwell Brig**, he was captured at **Airdsmoss** and executed on July 30th 1680 in Edinburgh.

The covenanters buried a few hundred yards from the monument were simply unfortunate prisoners from the Battle of Bothwell Brig who had played no part in the murder. They were hanged in chains on Magus Muir, after refusing to swear an oath not to rebel again. Bothwell Brig was the end of the resistance of the covenanters, 700 of whom were killed during the battle.

Over three hundred years later Sharp still seems to have enemies: someone has deliberately chipped his surname off the monument.

Follow the path behind the monument through the wood and it leads back to the start of the walk.

9

CRAIL TO FIFE NESS

Harbour
Castle Walk
Old Tolbooth
Museum
Parish Church
Old Airfield
Danes Dyke
Pill-boxes
Constantine's Cave

Staring Point: **The Harbour**

Directions to Start
A917 south from St Andrews

Opening Times
Crail Museum:
Summer 10am-12.30pm, 2.30-5pm Mon-Sat
2.30-5pm Sunday
Winter: weekends only

Guided walks: from Crail Museum 2.30pm
every Sunday (weather permitting) from
end of June to end of August.

Recommended Map
Ordnance Survey Landranger 59,
East Neuk & Largo Street Plan (2nd Edition)

Distance: 3 miles

The Harbour (1) is situated at the bottom of the extremely steep and ancient Shoregate, which is lined with well preserved crowstepped 17th and 18th century houses. The building with the large studded doors and the carving of a ship used to be the Custom House, headquarters of the local excisemen in the days when smuggling was widespread along the Fife coast.

The harbour itself is very old—the fishing industry in this part of the Fife coast was thriving as early as the reign of **David I** (1124-1153) and the harbour almost certainly existed at that time. A certain amount of rebuilding work was carried out in the 16th and 17th centuries; although by the start of the 18th century the harbour was in a fairly advanced state of disrepair as a result of a great storm in the winter of 1707. The upheavals of the 1650's—especially the activities of Cromwell's troops—may also have contributed to this lack of attention to the fabric of the harbour, and by 1656 Crail had only one ship left.

The oldest part of the harbour is the East Pier, with its stones placed vertically in the traditional local fashion. This pier was the most badly damaged in 1707 and it was not until the 1720's that it was repaired. The West Pier was designed by **Robert Stevenson** and completed in 1828 at a cost of just over £1,000.

From the harbour walk back up Shoregate and go up the short flight of steps on the corner just before it turns left towards the High Street. Walk along beneath the high walls of Castle Terrace until you come to the Turret on the corner. This is a Victorian gazebo, but it marks the site of Crail Castle.

Crail Castle stood just inside these walls, and it was used as a Royal residence by David I in the 12th century. It is said to have collapsed and fallen into the sea at some unspecified date. From this point on the corner of Castle Walk there are excellent views of the harbour and the coast to the south, as well as across to the Isle of May.

*Continue along Castle Walk and then along the Nethergate to Tolbooth Wynd. Turn left into Tolbooth Wynd and walk up to the junction of the High Street and Marketgate. Just around the corner to the right in Marketgate is the **Old Tolbooth (2)**.*

The Old Tolbooth, with its unusual pagoda-style roof, was built in the 16th century and its Dutch influenced design was a result of Crail's trading links with the Netherlands—Crail may have been exporting salt fish to the Netherlands as early as the 9th century. The tower, which houses an ancient bell with the Dutch inscription 'I was cast in the year of our Lord 1520', was altered in the late 18th century with the addition of a number of windows. The Tolbooth's gilded weather cock depicts a 'Crail Capon'—a form of dried or smoked haddock which was once a major export.

A little further along Marketgate on the right is the **Mercat Cross**. This cross dates from the 17th century, although it has only stood here since 1887 when it was renovated as part of the celebrations of Queen Victoria's Golden Jubilee.

Behind the Tolbooth is **Crail Museum (3)**. The Museum houses a collection of exhibits ranging from a 17th century oak charter chest to the last barber's pole in Crail. The many wrecks from the

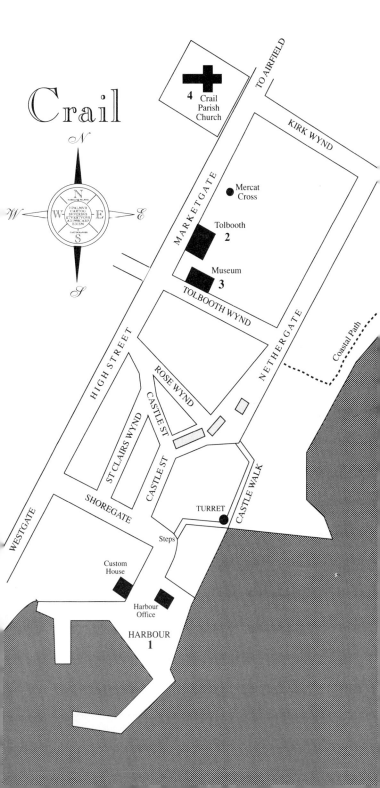

Crail

N

W · E

S

TO AIRFIELD

KIRK WYND

4 Crail Parish Church

Mercat Cross

Tolbooth **2**

Museum **3**

MARKETGATE

TOLBOOTH WYND

NETHERGATE

Coastal Path

HIGH STREET

ROSE WYND

CASTLE ST

ST CLAIRS WYND

CASTLE ST

SHOREGATE

CASTLE WALK

TURRET

Steps

WESTGATE

Custom House

Harbour Office

HARBOUR 1

coast around Crail are commemorated in a display highlighting the work of local lifeboatmen, including the rescue of 54 seamen from the wreck of *HMS Success* by Coxswain Andrew Cunningham and his crew in December 1914. The upper floor houses a fascinating collection of memorabilia relating to the wartime airfield, *HMS Jackdaw*, the remains of which can still be seen just outside the town. The collection includes the Commanding Officer's chair, an ancient flying jacket and a collection of photographs and models—nearly all of which were donated by people who served at the airfield during the Second World War.

Continue along Marketgate to **Crail Parish Church (4)**.

Crail Parish Church dates back to at least 1177 and it was dedicated to St Maelrubha by Bishop David de Bernham of St Andrews in 1243. Along with other churches along the Fife coast, its revenues originally belonged to the Cistercian nuns of Haddington, but at the start of the 16th century it became a wealthy collegiate church full of 'ornamentis and sylver werk', Sir William Myreton having founded the altar of St Michael the Archangel in 1512. By 1517 there were nine such altars in the church, and by this time the church had come to be known as St Marys.

John Knox preached in the church in May 1559, although on this occasion his sermon did not inspire the congregation to the sort of destruction that took place in St Andrews after his appearance at Holy Trinity Church in June of that year.

Here lyes interr'd before this tomb
The corpse of Bailie Thomas Young
An honest man of good renown
Was . . . tines a Bailie in this town
. . . several years Convener . . .
. . . . into the dust . . . . . .
. . . 20th of October Born . . . .
. . . . . . in 1683
. . . . d December . . . . . . d . . . . ht
. . . . no 1759
. . . with great composure of this l . .
. . . in the . . . year of his . . . e
. . . el Makmans spouse . . . . . . here
. . . also . . . of their children dead

IPX

James Sharp, who later became Archbishop of St Andrews, was minister here in the late 1640's.

The original Norman building had its chancel lengthened and a stone spire added in the 16th century, further alterations being made in 1796, 1815 and 1828. The interior was renovated in 1963. A 9th century Celtic cross and the tombstone of Sir James Ewart, a 16th century collegiate chaplain, are preserved in the porch.

The Churchyard contains a large number of elaborate 17th and 18th century tombs. In the eastern corner you will find the headless figure of a knight, in early 17th century armour, standing between Corinthian pillars decorated with skulls and trophies. This is probably **William Bruce of Symbister** who died around 1630. Close to this tomb is a strange weather-beaten column, its inscription having long since disappeared. On the north side of the churchyard is an extremely grim-looking Mort House, with the inscription:

ERECTED *for securing the* DEAD :
ANN: DOM: MDCCCXXVI

Built in 1826, it was intended to thwart the ambitions of grave-robbers.

To the east of the church are the graves of three airmen who were killed in flying accidents at the nearby airfield in the winter of 1918: Lt Clarence Reginald Mundy, Air Mechanic F. Green, and Flt Cadet J.A. Scarratt. In the modern extension to the churchyard just north of the church are the graves of those who died at *HMS Jackdaw* during the Second World War—many of them having lost their lives while taking part in dangerous low-level training near the Isle of May.

Close to the gates of the church is the **'Blue Stone'**— a boulder which, according to legend, was thrown across from the Isle of May by the Devil in a failed attempt to disrupt the building of the church.

Leave the church and continue along to the end of Marketgate where it joins the Balcomie Road. Follow this road for about one mile until you see the **old airfield** *on the right.*

This abandoned airfield, which was known as *HMS Jackdaw* during the Second World War, still retains many of its original buildings, including the control tower. During the Second World War, the airfield became a Royal Naval Air Station defending the approaches to the Forth, and at one time more than 3,000 people were stationed here. 785 Squadron, who arrived in 1940, were originally equipped with the rather antique Swordfish Torpedo bombers of the type that were to be instrumental in the sinking of the *Bismarck*. A Letter to the *Daily Telegraph* in March 1991 described an encounter with two of these aircraft near Crail in 1940:

Sir,
An Austin Seven has overtaken a Tiger Moth (letter, March 21), but in 1940 two cyclists overtook two Swordfish aircraft flying into a 30-knot wind on the road west of Crail, Fife. Jock McLellan, a fellow St Andrews student, and I were resting on top of a long brae when the Fleet Air Arm planes came hovering overhead along the line of the road. By pedalling furiously downhill for a

quarter of a mile we overtook them.
Credit goes to gravity.
G. Rankine, Petersfield, Hants

785 Squadron flew Sharks as well as Swordfishes, and as the war progressed all sorts of aircraft were flown from here—including Barracudas, Aircobras, Walruses, Sea-Hurricanes and Hampdens. The Hampdens, which took part in the sinking of the *Tirpitz* in a Norwegian fjord in 1944, were variously known as 'potato mashers', 'flying suitcases' and 'sardine tins'—because of their unusual shape and the problems encountered when attempting to bale out of one.

The station commander appears to have been very particular about the state of the grass on the airfield. On one occasion, a pilot coming back from Norway crash-landed his badly shot up Hudson bomber just off the runway, and instead of being congratulated on his survival, he was severely reprimanded for making a mess of the grass.

Continue along this road, passing **Balcomie Castle**, *once the home of the 18th century gambler General John Scott (see Kilrenny Walk), just off the road on the left.*

Balcomie Castle was built in the late 16th century by the Learmonth family, but most of it was demolished around 1800 to make way for a farmhouse. In 1705 Balcomie was purchased by **Sir William Hope** of Kirkliston. Sir William was an experienced soldier and one of the finest swordsmen of his time. He wrote a highly successful book on the subject entitled *The Complete Fencing Master*, which was published in 1686 and included instructions on the use of the small-sword and single combat on horseback. Not long after Sir William took up residence at Balcomie, a French swordsman who had read the book arrived in Crail intending to challenge Sir William to a duel. The duel was fought on horseback in a field close to the road less than a mile from Balcomie, where, after a long drawn out struggle, Sir William killed the Frenchman.

Sir William was also well known as an accomplished dancer, and he is said to have died in 1724 of a fever brought on by dancing the minuet. Balcomie was bought by **General John Scott** in 1766, who carried out a certain amount of rebuilding and lived here in great style, even employing a French chef, one Monsieur Baile.

> *The road ends at Balcomie Links, home of the Crail Golfing Society which was founded in 1786 and is the seventh oldest golf club in the world. A path leads from the car park and continues alongside the raised wall of **Dane's Dyke**, which leads down to the coast at **Fife Ness**.*

Dane's Dyke is partly natural and partly man made and used to enclose Fife Ness. Its exact connection with Viking raiders is unknown, although it probably takes its name from the **'Long Man's Grave'**, the tomb of a Viking warrior which was popularly believed to be sited at the sea end of the dyke. No trace of it can be seen today.

> *From the end of Dane's Dyke follow the coastal path around to the **Coastguard Station**.*

Just below the Coastguard Station is a Second World War pill-box, cunningly disguised to look like a dry stone wall. A little further around the coast is the natural harbour where **Mary of Guise** (1515-1560) landed in June 1538. She rested at Balcomie Castle before going on to St Andrews, where she married **James V** in the cathedral the following day. Their only child, Mary, was born on the 8th of December 1542 and became Queen of Scotland one week later after the sudden death of James V at Falkland Palace. During the minority of her daughter, Mary of Guise was involved in all manner of intrigue intended to further the **'Auld Alliance'** between Scotland and France and to thwart the ambitions of the English—in particular Henry VIII's plan to dominate Scotland through the marriage of his heir to the infant Queen of Scotland. Mary eventually managed to arrange for her daughter to marry the French Dauphin in 1558. Mary of Guise used her powers as Regent to institute a campaign against Protestant 'heretics'—one of the victims was **Walter Myln**, who is commemorated on the Martyrs Monument in St Andrews—and this led to open conflict with the Protestant forces of the **Lords of the Congregation**. Despite assistance from French forces who landed at Leith, Mary was unable to defeat her enemies and died, with the conflict still unresolved, in Edinburgh Castle on the 11th of June 1560.

The path continues above the beach, skirting the golf course, and just beside the path, in front of the clubhouse is a well-concealed sniping post. Another relic from the start of the Second World War when a German invasion was a very real possibility, this strongpoint, constructed from steel plates buried in the bank at the edge of the beach, would only have accommodated one man—and his chances of survival would have been very limited had the invasion become a reality.

*Continue along the path, through the fragmentary remains of what seems to have been another large pill-box, until you reach **Constantine's Cave**.*

This is the cave where **Constantine II**, King of Alba in the middle of the 9th century, is believed to have been killed by the Danes sometime around 877. The walls of the cave are decorated with small Celtic crosses, which are now very indistinct but can still be seen.

Return to Crail either by the same route, or along the coastal path.

10

ANSTRUTHER AND CELLARDYKE

The Shell House
Anstruther Wester Churchyard
St Adrian's Parish Church
Cellardyke Harbour
Caiplie Caves
Billowness

Starting Point: The Shell House
on Elizabeth Place, opposite
Anstruther Wester Church

Directions to Start
A917 south from St Andrews, and continue
through Crail

Opening Times
Scottish Fisheries Museum:
Summer 10am-5.30pm; Sundays 11am-5pm;
Winter 10am-4.30pm; Sundays 2-4.pm.

North Carr Lightship: Summer 11am-5pm;
For winter opening, check with the tourist
information office (0334 72021).

Recommended Maps
Ordnance Survey Landranger 59
East Neuk & Largo Street Plan (2nd Edition)

Distance: Town walk 1 mile;
Cellardyke & Caves 4 miles; Billowness 3 miles

Anstruther Wester Church

The Shell House (1), or Buckie House as it is also
known, was built in the 1690's and was once the
home of **Alexander Batchelor**, a slater and well
known local eccentric who decorated the outside of
the house with shells. The present design on the
wall facing the church is a fairly recent (1968) renovation of Batchelor's original work. **Robert Louis
Stevenson**, who stayed in Anstruther in 1868 when
his father was working on the new harbour, described the house thus:

> 'This had been the residence of an
> agreeable eccentric; during his fond
> tenancy, he had illustrated the outer
> walls as high as the roof, with elaborate
> patterns, and pictures, and snatches of
> verse; shells and pebbles artfully
> contrasted and conjoined had

been his medium; and I like to think of
him standing back upon the bridge,
when all was finished, drinking in the
general effect.'

Some of the rooms were decorated in a similar
fashion, and Batchelor even charged 3d admission
to those who wished to see the interior of the house.
Batchelor died in 1866, but took his obsession with
him to the grave, as he had designed a coffin decorated just like his house.

Cross the road and go into the churchyard.

Anstruther Wester Church (2) comprises a 16th
century steeple and what may once have been a
building of considerable antiquity, although the
rebuilding work done in the mid 18th and 19th
centuries has left no visible sign of this earlier
building. It is now used as a church hall. The most
interesting external feature is the plaque dated 1598
that can still be seen on the south wall depicting two
Romanesque archways and bearing the inscription:

ENTER IN AT YE STRAIT GET
IT IS YE VYD GET YAT LEDS TO PERDITION

A little further along is the grave of an 'unknown
seaman of the Great War' and a stone coffin that is
reputed to have miraculously floated over from the
Isle of May carrying the body of **St Adrian**, who had
been killed by Viking raiders around 875. There are
also a number of other interesting stones, including
one of 1786 with a carving of a ship. The churchyard
slopes down to the sea and there are good views
across the old harbour, once overshadowed by the
battlements of Dreel Castle, towards the new har-

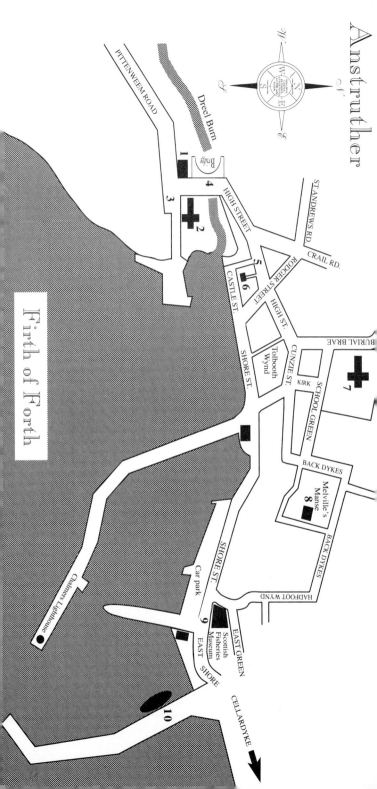

Anstruther

Firth of Forth

PITTENWEEM ROAD

Dreel Burn

Bridge

1
3
4
2

HIGH STREET

ST. ANDREWS RD.

CRAIL RD.

5
6

CASTLE ST.

ROGER STREET

HIGH ST.

SHORE ST.

Tolbooth Wynd

CUNZIE ST.

KIRK

BURIAL BRAE

7

SCHOOL GREEN

BACK DYKES

Melville's Manse

8

BACK DYKES

HADFOOT WYND

Chalmers Lighthouse

Car park

SHORE ST.

9

Scottish Fisheries Museum

EAST GREEN

EAST SHORE

CELLARDYKE

10

bour. The engineer in charge of the building of the new harbour in 1868 was the father of Robert Louis Stevenson:

> 'Only one thing in connection with that harbour tempted me, and that was diving, an experience I burned to taste of. But this was not to be, at least in Anstruther.'
> **R. L. Stevenson**

Leaving the churchyard, just across the road to the left is the house of **Captain John Keay (3)**.

Keay was well known as the Captain of the tea clipper *Ariel* which held the record for a sailing ship from Gravesend to Hong Kong—he took 83 days. In 1859 Keay brought his clipper *Ellen Rodger* home first in the tea race from China to London. In the same race in 1866 as Captain of the *Ariel* Keay was involved in a titanic struggle with the clipper *Taeping*, and was finally beaten by only 20 minutes after a voyage that had lasted 99 days.

Continue by crossing the bridge over the Dreel Burn and follow the High Street round to the right.

This bridge over the **Dreel Burn (4)** was built in 1630 and rebuilt in 1795 and 1831. These dates are still to be seen on the bridge next to the three fish crest of Anstruther Wester.

The Dreel was often used by smugglers who operated in the area, as it provided them with a convenient route to bring goods inland from the coast. Caves on the Isle of May were used to store wine, tobacco and cloth, and even the manse was reputed to have a concealed passage leading down to the

Wightman's Wynd

sea. Andrew Wilson and his accomplice George Robertson, who later became the focus of the **Porteous Riot** in Edinburgh in 1736, were smugglers in this area and were finally caught after robbing an exciseman who was staying in St Mary Street in Pittenweem. *(See Pittenweem Walk.)*

> *On the south side of the High Street is the now rather gloomy and dilapidated* **Wightman's Wynd (5)**.

This wynd takes its name from Charles Wightman who lived here in the middle of the 18th century. The ruinous tower and walling at the bottom of the wynd are all that remain of his house. He apparently spread the story that his house was haunted by a 'black lady' as a cover for his smuggling and

Jacobite activities. In 1745, for example, he hid fugitives from the Battle of Culloden here until they could escape to France.

A few yards further up High St is Old Post Office Close, at the end of which was the home of **Thomas Chalmers** *(1780-1847)* **(6)**.

Chalmers, 'a solar man who drew after him a firmament of planets', was born in Anstruther in 1780 and began his studies at St Andrews University when he was only 11. He was made Professor of Moral Philosophy there in 1823. Later he became Professor of Theology at Edinburgh, and in 1843 was the first moderator of the breakaway Free Church of Scotland.

> 'In spite of a bad figure, voice, gesture and look, and an unusual plainness of Scotch accent, Chalmers is a great orator, at the moment of speaking, unapproached in our day. I have often hung upon his words with a beating heart and a tearful eye, without being brought to my senses till I read next day the syllables that had moved me to admiration, but which then seemed cold.'
> **Lord Cockburn**

Chalmers, as well as being a consummate orator, maintained a lifelong interest in mathematics, and he is even said to have regulated the strokes of his razor when shaving according to a mathematical formula. When he died in May 1847 he was the most eminent Scottish minister of his time, and more than 100,000 people lined the streets of Edinburgh to see his funeral procession pass by.

Continue along High Street to the junction with Rodger Street. At the junction, high up on the wall of the large house is a good example of a marriage lintel. These were plaques placed over the doors of houses to commemorate the marriage of the owners. This one was that of Robert Alexander and his wife Christian—he represented Anstruther in the Scottish Parliament of 1631. Continue along to the house of **William Tennant** *(1784-1848) on the left.*

Tennant was the author of the poem *Anster Fair* and was a noted scholar, eventually becoming Professor of Oriental Languages at St Andrews in 1843. He was also a founder member of the *Musomanik Society* , a sort of poets drinking club, which included **Sir Walter Scott** and **James Hogg**, the Ettrick Shepherd, amongst its members.

At the end of High Street you will come to the junction of Burial Brae (up the hill to the left) and **Cunzie St**, *to the right. Cunzie Street is where Cromwell's troops were billeted in the 1650's as a result of the town's support for Charles II. Turn left up Burial Brae and continue up to the gate into the church.*

St Adrian's Parish Church (7) was begun in 1634 and finished in 1644; although it was substantially altered in the 1830's. It replaced Kilrenny as the local parish church after complaints about the hardship of marching out to Kilrenny 'a mile distant of deep evil way in winter and rainy times'. The first minister was Colin Adam who arrived from Kilrenny in 1641.

On the south wall of the church are a number of interesting monuments. One, marked 1834 and placed in a blocked doorway, reads:

which probably derived from the 1598 inscription at Anstruther Wester Church. A little further along this wall is a memorial to a most unusual local resident, Tetuanuireiaiteraiatea, **Princess Titaua Marama of Tahiti**. Born at Papetoai Moorea, Society Islands on 3rd November 1842, she was half English and had married **George Darsie** in Tahiti in 1878 before returning with him to live in Anstruther. She remained in Anstruther till her death in September 1898. Her daughter Paloma is also buried here.

On the east wall of the church is a memorial to **Captain James Black**, Knight of the Bath and Knight of the Imperial Order of Maria Theresa, who died in December 1835. Black became famous as a result of his gallantry at the battle of Trafalgar in 1805, when in true seafaring tradition he nailed his colours to the mast of his ship *Mars* as a sign to his crew that there was no question of surrender under any circumstances.

In 1807 while in command of the *Eighty Four*, Black was caught in a storm while at anchor off Yarmouth. The ship seemed certain to run aground and be wrecked until Black took decisive action. With the help of a few volunteers, he cut away the masts and the ship was saved. In 1813 Black became Captain of *HMS Weasel* and fought a number of actions against the French. His house, *Marsfield*, can still be seen next to the golf club at the south end of Shore Road.

Just to the right of Black's memorial is a curious monument erected by Captain David Henderson, master of the excise yacht *Prince of Wales* in 1813. **George Gourlay** (1832-1891), the Anstruther bookseller and local historian, described the *Prince of Wales* thus in his book *Fisher Life or the Memorials of Cellardyke* published in 1879:

> '[in 1800] smugglers were almost
> nightly on the coast, running their
> cargoes amongst the rocks skirting St
> Andrews; but however alert, and often
> on the track, the old brig was but a
> lame dog in the chase.'

Depicting a sailing ship within an elaborate wooden frame, the ravages of time and the weather have eroded the name and details of the person to whom this stone was dedicated. Henderson's own grave is nearby.

> *On leaving the churchyard go back down Burial*
> *Brae and turn left into School Green. Continue*
> *along to the end of School Green and then go into*
> *the high-walled lane directly ahead that leads*
> *around the back of* **Melville's Manse (8)** *and into*
> *Back Dykes.*

Melville's Manse was built in the 1590's and is named after **James Melville** who came to Anstruther as minister in 1586. In 1588 Melville's leadership of the local community was severely tested when a ship of the Spanish Armada landed at Anstruther under the command of **Jan Gomez de Medina**, its crew in a 'Maist miserable and pitiful condition'. They were the survivors of a number of ships that had been wrecked off the Orkneys, as Melville wrote:

'The Lord of armies, wha ryddes upon
the wings of the winds, was in the
mean tyme convoying that monstrous
navie about our costes, and directing
their hulks and galiates to the ylands,
rokkes, and sands, wharupon he had
destinat their wrak and destruction.'

Having been woken with the news that 'Spainyarts'
had landed at the harbour, Melville set out to meet
them. This is his own account of that meeting:

'assembling the honest men of toun, [I]
cam to the Tolbuthe; and efter
consultation taken to heir tham, and
what answer to mak, ther presentes us
a verie reverend man of big stature,
and grave and stour countenance, grey-
bearded, and verie humble lyk, wha,
efter mikle and verie law courtessie,
bowing down with his face neir the
ground, and twiching my scho with
his hand, began his harang in the
Spanise toung, wharof I understud the
substance.'

Melville agreed to help them in order to demon-
strate 'the superiority of the Protestant religion'.
The soldiers and sailors—'young berdless men,
sillie, trauchled, and houngered', of whom there
were about 250, were allowed ashore and fed, while
the officers were entertained in rather better style
by **Sir James Anstruther**. After his return to Spain,
Gomez de Medina showed his gratitude by person-
ally securing the release of the crew of an Anstruther
boat that had been arrested in a Spanish port.

*From Back Dykes head east to Haddfoot Wynd and
turn right, passing the site of the now demolished*

*Chalmers Memorial Church on the left. Continue
down the hill towards the harbour until you come
to the Scottish Fisheries Museum on the corner.*

The Scottish Fisheries Museum (9) is housed in a
group of historic buildings, known as St Ayles,
close to the harbour. The last owners of St Ayles
before it became a museum were the Cunningham
family who ran a ships chandlers and also used the
courtyard to dry and mend fishing nets. The museum houses a wide collection of artefacts and
displays connected with the fishing industry – from
models of fishing boats to a replica of a fisherman's
garret. It also houses the *Memorial to Scottish Fishermen Lost at Sea.*

Moored against the east wall of the harbour not far
from the museum is the **North Carr Lightship (10)**.
This was the last lightship in Scotland and was
stationed off the Fife coast at the North Carr rocks
from 1933 to 1975. It is now open to the public as a
lighthouse museum.

*From here there are two alternatives for those
wishing to extend this walk:*

1
Cellardyke to Caiplie Caves

From the Scottish Fisheries Museum head east to Cellardyke harbour along East Green, James Street, George Street and Shore Street.

Cellardyke got its name from the rows of cellars built here by the men of Kilrenny to store their nets close to the shore. The harbour itself was built in the 1570's and altered in the mid 19th century, and has been the scene of many dramatic incidents over the years.

One of the 'saddest tragedies that ever occurred on the Fifeshire coast' took place here on the 23rd September 1793. **Alexander Wood**, a descendant of Admiral Sir Andrew Wood of Largo and at one time house carpenter for General John Scott of Balcomie, and six companions were forced to go to sea in stormy weather in order to save their nets which were anchored not far from the shore:

> 'Still they were seen to hesitate before they began to climb down the rugged pier to gain the boat; but remembering what they had to secure in the way of home comforts they at last pushed to sea. Most of them were landsmen, but the oars were plied so well that they had reached the outside of the skerries. The danger, indeed, was seemingly passed, when a great wave rose, like a ruthless enemy, and with scarce a moments warning hurled her back upon the beacon rock. A weary cry echoes along the beach, to which the

neighbours rush in breathless haste in all directions. "A boat, a boat!" shouts an excited voice, and a hundred willing hands spring responsive to the call. But the task is in vain, and brave men stand still in anguish and despair....the struggle is short and decisive; one strong swimmer flings his arms in the air and disappears forever. Two bosom friends cling together on the broken gunwale; but what is devotion and sacrifice to the pitiless surge? and they die together. A firm foot has gained a rock; but the enemy is on his trail, and the hapless fisher rolls back a bleeding and bruised corpse; and so the crew one by one perished, with the solitary exception of the youth James Martin, who is borne up amidst all the death and terror of the storm, as if an angel hand had been outstretched for his deliverance, till he landed unharmed on the high rock to the leeward of the harbour.'

George Gourlay
Memorials of Cellardyke (1879)

James Martin 'an honest and deserving man' went back to sea and died of cholera at Wick in 1832. Coincidentally, a similar tragedy occurred at Cellardyke in 1800, and again only one man survived to tell the tale. He was **William Watson**, 'a fine specimen of a Scottish fisherman, one whose courage and endurance was as conspicuous as his strength and activity'. He was known as 'Water Willie' in remembrance of his remarkable escape:

'"I felt as if I walked on the water", he told his friends, and so it seemed to

others, so strangely was he borne on
the great billow that swept him to the
shore.'

His own wife apparently pulled him from the water, and he lived another 50 years, dying in February 1850 aged 77.

At this point it may be worth noting a few local fishing traditions: it is generally regarded to be bad luck to refer to a minister, a pig or a salmon on a fishing boat, so the minister is known as 'the queer fellow', a pig is as a 'curlytail', and a salmon as 'the silver beastie'. It is also bad luck to meet a minister on the way to the boat, or to go to sea on a Friday.

Continue along the coast to the bathing pool, just below the war memorial.

This was this the site of the 'Cardinal's Steps'—where **Cardinal David Beaton** *(see Walk 1—The Castle)* is said to have landed in his state barge when he was staying in Anstruther. The Beaton's were an important local family who owned land in this area, and David Beaton may have been buried at Kilrenny after his murder in St Andrews; although it is thought more likely he was buried in Blackfriars Chapel in St Andrews.

*Walk east along the coast about one and a half miles until you come to **Caiplie Caves**.*

The largest of these caves, known as **Chapel Cave**, shows signs of human habitation, possibly by followers of **St Adrian**. A door appears to have been cut through into an adjacent cave on the western side. At the rear of Chapel Cave is a small inner cave, apparently with crosses carved around the entrance—although you will need a good torch to spot these, as the authors were unable to find them when they visited the caves. An excavation here in 1841 uncovered human remains; possibly those of primitive hunters dating back to c.2000 BC.

Return to Anstruther by the same route.

2
Shore Street to Billowness

From the Scottish Fisheries Museum head west along Shore Street to the Old Harbour. Turn right up Wightman's Wynd, left into the High Street, back across the Dreel Bridge and right onto the Pittenweem High Road. Take the first left into Crichton Street and then the first right into Shore Road. Follow the coast from here to **Billowness***.*

Billowness has a rather unhappy history—it was the place where witches were burned in the 17th century: Eppie Laing and two others who were alleged to have called up the storm in which the architect of the first lighthouse on the Isle of May was drowned were burned here.

When the plague arrived in Crail in 1645 the town council of Anstruther proclaimed on 17th November:

> 'Ye nybor burgh of Carrael is infecit
> with ye pestilence, they ordaine ye haill
> back yetts and vennells of this burgh to
> be closit, and ye ports to be keipit bothe
> night and day, and non of ye
> inhabitants of ye burgh of Carrael to be
> recavit within this burgh.'

But the plague got through despite these precautions, and those local people who were unfortunate enough to fall victim were thrown out of the town and left to die on Billowness. More than 70 people died here during that outbreak of plague.

From here return to the town by the same route.

11

KILRENNY

Kilrenny Church
Scott Mausoleum
Lumsdaine Tomb
Innergellie
Kilrenny Common

Starting Point: Kilrenny Church

Directions to Start
A917 coast road through Crail
towards Anstruther

Recommended Maps
Ordnance Survey Landranger 59,
East Neuk & Largo Street Plan (2nd Edition)

Distance: 1 mile

General Scott's Tomb

Kilrenny Church (1) dates from the 15th century, although only the tower has survived from this period, the rest of the church having been rebuilt in the 19th century. The churchyard contains a number of notable tombs, the largest of which is that of **General John Scott of Balcomie**, a descendant of Sir John Scot of Scotstarvit *(see Hill of Tarvit Walk)*, who died in 1775. This massive, gloomy mausoleum in the north west corner, with its ribbed and arched roof, gives no hint of the life of its occupant, who was one of the most successful gamblers of the 18th century.

After making his fortune while serving in India—some said as a direct result of acquiring a large quantity of plundered rubies—Scott amassed over half a million pounds by gambling. His most

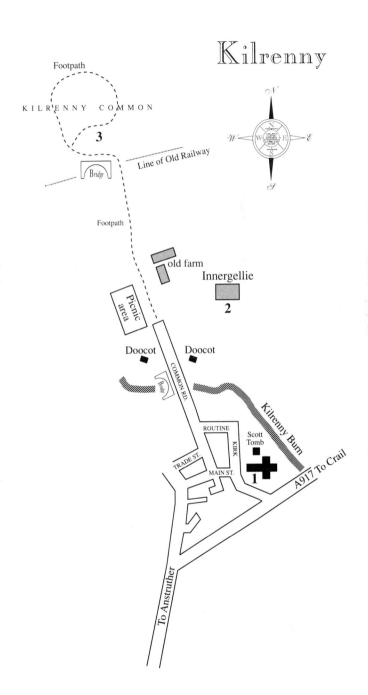

Kilrenny

Footpath

KILRENNY COMMON

3

Line of Old Railway

Bridge

Footpath

old farm

Innergellie

2

Picnic area

Doocot   Doocot

COMMON RD.

Bridge

ROUTINE

Kilrenny Burn

Scott Tomb

KIRK

TRADE ST.

1

MAIN ST.

A917 To Crail

To Anstruther

celebrated wager was £30,000 against the house of **Sir Lawrence Dundas** in St Andrew Square in Edinburgh (now the Royal Bank of Scotland). Dundas unwisely took the bet and promptly lost his house. Scott allowed Dundas to retain the house; but in exchange Dundas had to build another similar house at a site of Scott's choosing. This house was built at Bellevue in Edinburgh and later became a Customs House.

When General Scott died in 1775, he left each of his three daughters more than £100,000. The eldest, Henrietta, married the Duke of Portland; the second daughter, Lucy, became Countess of Moray; and the third, Johanna, married **George Canning**, who later became Prime Minister. Henrietta later added to her already considerable fortune when, in 1815, she sold the Isle of May to the Commissioners for Northern Lighthouses for £60,000.

On the western side of the church tower is the monument of **Lumsdaine of Innergellie** (Innergellie being the estate to the north of the village). This well worn Georgian tomb probably dates from 1823—the date on the armorial stone between the Doric columns.

Innergellie was purchased by **Sir James Lumsdaine** in the 1630's. He was another Scot who, like his comrade in arms **David Leslie** of Newark Castle, had fought for Gustavus Adolphus in the 30 Years War, taking part in the battles of Frankfurt and Leipzig. He returned to Scotland and led the defence of Dundee against **General Monk** during the siege of 1651. After the town was forced to surrender Lumsdaine was murdered, even though he had been promised quarter.

Close to the north wall of the church is a stone dated 1672, commemorating Robert Ford, and depicting a ship of the 17th century under full sail. It is said that **Cardinal David Beaton** may have been buried at Kilrenny after his murder in St Andrews Castle, but it seems more likely that he was buried in Blackfriars Chapel in St Andrews.

> *From the churchyard turn right into Kirk Wynd and then left into Routine Row until it joins the Common Road. Turn right and head up the track between the two Dovecots. Just past the Dovecots on the right is **Innergellie House (2)**, built in the 1760's, and close to the path are the ruins of an elaborate 19th century farm. From here continue on to **Kilrenny Common (3)**. The path forms a short circular walk around the wooded common, over an old railway bridge and then back to Kilrenny.*

From the northern end of the common you can see a number of farms, and the one about a mile to the north east is called Thirdpart. In the 14th century, the **Laird of Thirdpart** got into a dispute with **Sir William Anstruther**, who had built Dreel Castle in Anstruther. The dispute arose because Anstruther had rejected Thirdpart as a suitor for his eldest daughter. Thirdpart plotted to poison Anstruther at a dinner he was giving, but as Anstruther rode to Thirdpart he was warned of the danger by a beggar he met at a bridge and returned home. Anstruther then invited Thirdpart to visit him at Dreel Castle the next day.

> 'Sir William met him in the courtyard of Dreel as he was alighting from his horse, but when he advanced to enter the tower, the Knight, placing himself on the doorstep, challenged him as a

115

true man to clear himself from the imputation of treachery, at the same time calling on the beggar to repeat his story. Thirdpart's brow darkened and his lips grew livid, as he listened to the tale, and before it was concluded he made an effort to speak, but the words 'liar and traitor' were all that he could utter. The hot temper of the Knight of Dreel, already chafed by a night's meditation on the toils that had been laid for him under the mask of friendship, now burst forth with ungovernable fury. 'Traitor is he?' roared the Knight; 'nay, thou art the traitor', and with one step backward he reached his trusty poleaxe from the wall, and with a single blow clove his opponent's skull on his own threshold.'

Rev Walter Wood
The East Neuk of Fife
Its History and Antiquities (1881)

Anstruther soon regretted his hasty action, and only a Royal pardon saved him from execution. It is said that soon afterwards he changed his heraldic crest to two hands holding a poleaxe with the motto *'Periissem ni periissem'* or 'I had perished had I not gone through with it.'

From Kilrenny it is possible to cross the main road (A917) and head straight down to the coast at the Cardinal's Steps, and then continue along the coast to Caiplie Caves (see Anstruther and Cellardyke Walk).

12

PITTENWEEM

Parish Church
Tolbooth Tower
The Priory
St Fillans Cave
The Harbour
Kellie Lodging

Starting Point: The Parish Church on Kirkgate,
at the north east end of the High Street.

Directions to Start
A917 south from St Andrews, and turn onto the
B9131 to Anstruther. At Anstruther rejoin the
A917 south west to Pittenweem

Opening Times
The key to St Fillan's Cave can be obtained from
The Gingerbread Horse (craft & teashop), 9 High
St. Admission: 25p. The key to the Parish Church
can be obtained from Campbell's Chemist Shop,
Market Place during shop hours.

Recommended Maps
East Neuk & Largo Street Plan (2nd edition)
Ordnance Survey Landranger 59

Distance: 1 mile

Tearooms
The Gingerbread Horse, 9 High St
Tearoom & Coffee bar, Mid Shore

Pittenweem Parish Church (1) is a curious building, being a combination of a church and the old Tolbooth. The tower at the western gable end was originally the town Tolbooth and it served as both a meeting place for the town council and as a prison—in the 18th century the Pittenweem witches are said to have been held here before being burned at the stake in the Priory garden.

Although most of the present church was built in the 1580's, recent renovation work has uncovered evidence that some parts of the structure date back to the 12th century. This suggests that there was a church on this site even before the building of the 13th century priory, which stands just to the south east of the church in Cove Wynd.

The Tolbooth Tower also dates from the 1580's, although the spire is a 17th century addition and the clock is a nineteenth century replacement for one built in 1773 by John Smith, a local watchmaker who is buried in the churchyard.

The Churchyard contains a number of interesting gravestones including that of David Binning, which is to the left of the gate as you come in:

HEIR LYETH THE CORPS OF A FAMOVS MAN
DAVID BINNING SKIPPER AND LATE BAILLIE
OF THIS BVRGH AND HVSBAND TO
AGNES ADAMSON WHO DEPARTED THE FIRST
OF SEPR 1675 HIS AGE 36

and Charles Moyes Esq, who died in 1842 aged 98 and was 'beloved of all who knew him for his cheerful and happy temper, kind and amiable disposition'.

The Tolbooth Tower

On leaving the churchyard turn left into Cove Wynd. Just past the Old Priory on the left is the entrance to St Fillan's Cave.

The Old Augustinian Priory (2) was originally established in the 13th century by monks from the Isle of May. The gatehouse was built in the 15th century and rebuilding continued through the centuries, the last major work being undertaken by **Sir Robert Lorimer** in 1921. The Priory is probably best known as the place where witches were burned in 1704-5, these macabre rituals taking place in the garden.

> 'Judges allow themselves too much
> liberty, in condemning such as are
> accused of this crime because they
> conclude they cannot be severe enough
> to the enemies of God; and Assizers are
> afraid to suffer such to escape as are

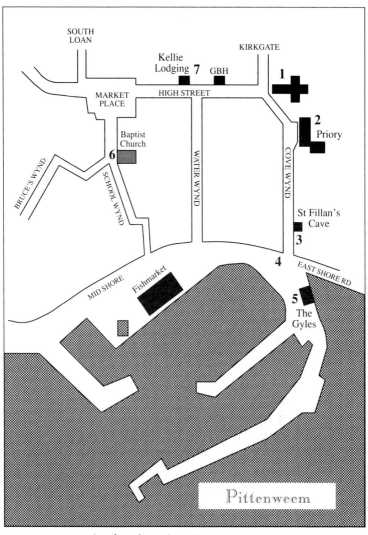

SOUTH LOAN

Kellie Lodging **7** GBH

KIRKGATE

MARKET PLACE

HIGH STREET

1

2 Priory

Baptist Church

6

COVE WYND

BRUCE'S WYND

SCHOOL WYND

WATER WYND

St Fillan's Cave

3

4

EAST SHORE RD

MID SHORE

Fishmarket

5 The Gyles

Pittenweem

remitted to them, lest they let loose an enraged Wizard in their neighbourhood. And thus poor Innocents die in multitudes by an unworthy martyrdom, and burning comes in fashion.'

Sir George Mackenzie 1672

121

Fishing villages often became involved in the 17th century witch hunt, and the search for a scapegoat for a disaster at sea often ended with a witchcraft accusation. East Lothian and Fife were particularly noted for this, while at Pittenweem one particular disaster seems to have been responsible for an outbreak of witch hunting when, in 1649, almost 100 local men did not return from the **Battle of Kilsyth**. The town was plunged into an immediate and marked decline, and the ensuing social tensions no doubt provided just the sort of spark required to make people look for supernatural reasons for their earthly problems.

Walk past the Priory down Cove Wynd towards the harbour and the entrance to St Fillan's Cave (3) is on the left. (If you want to go into the cave, you will find the key at The Gingerbread Horse, 9 High St.)

The name 'Pittenweem' is Pictish in origin and means 'place of the cave', thus the town itself is named after this cave. The cave takes its name from the 7th century Christian missionary, **St Fillan**, who is supposed to have lived in it, and in the middle ages it became a place of pilgrimage. Very little is known about St Fillan—he may have belonged to the **Culdees**, who had a small community on the Kirkhill in St Andrews—but the only tangible evidence of his existence are certain relics which are traditionally thought to have belonged to him. These are now preserved in the Royal Museum of Scotland in Edinburgh.

Once inside the cave you will see a flight of steps, possibly cut by Augustinian monks in the 12th century, that lead up a steep and narrow passage to the left of the entrance. This leads up to a damp,

The Gyles

barrel-vaulted chamber that is directly below the priory garden and is said to have been used by smugglers in the 18th century.

One of the best known smugglers of the time was **Andrew Wilson**, who was eventually ruined by the repeated seizures of his contraband by the excisemen. In September 1736, determined to get his revenge, he heard that **James Stark**, a Kirkcaldy customs officer, had come to Pittenweem with about £200 in his possession. With his accomplices he robbed Stark of the £200 while he was staying at a house at the west end of Marygate, not far from the parish church. Wilson and one of his accomplices, **George Robertson**, were both soon caught and sentenced to death. However, public opinion was very much on their side, especially after Wilson unselfishly helped Robertson to escape, and when Wilson was hanged in the Grassmarket in Edinburgh the crowd was so incensed that the Captain of the town guard, **John Porteous**, ordered his men to fire on them. Three were killed and many others injured. Porteous was condemned to death for his actions, but reprieved. The mob then took the law into their own hands and lynched Porteous in the Grassmarket. The full story is to be found in **Sir Walter Scott's** *Heart of Midlothian*.

The main body of the cave consists of two small chambers, one said to contain a well and the other occupied by a rough altar, built in the 1930's by the then Rector of Pittenweem, Rev W. H. de Voil. The cave is still occasionally used for religious services.

*Continue down Cove Wynd and onto the East Shore of **the harbour (4)**.*

The most striking feature of the harbour area is the group of buildings at its north east edge known as **The Gyles (5)**, which stand right on the rocks by the sea wall. Gyles House is the well preserved, white-washed house to the right and it was built in the early 17th century by **Captain James Cook**. Cook was the man who helped Charles II escape to France after the Battle of Worcester in 1651.

Most of the present harbour, with its fine pan-tile roofed houses, dates from the end of the 17th century, although there has been a harbour here since the 13th century, the outer harbour wall being the oldest part. In the 18th century the harbour served the salt and coal trading of **Sir John Anstruther**, and in the 19th century grain was one of the main commodities that passed through the harbour. It was not until the collapse of the grain trade towards the end of the 19th century that fishing really took over as the main industry in Pittenweem.

At the eastern end of the harbour are the houses that belonged to the sea captains, and you can still see where the hoists were used to lift tackle up into the lofts.

*Walk along the harbour until you reach School Wynd on the right, opposite the fish market. Go up School Wynd and stop at the **Baptist Church (6)**.*

Looking back towards the harbour from Bruce's Wynd, which joins School Wynd here, you get one of the best views of the town and its pantiled roofscape.

At the top of School Wynd turn right into the High Street.

The most significant building on the High Street is the **Kellie Lodging (7)**, which served as the town house for the Lords of Kellie Castle and was built in the late 16th century.

Continuing along the High Street, the Tolbooth tower marks the end of the walk.

13

ST MONANS CHURCH
TO NEWARK CASTLE

Old Church
Graveyard
Coastal walk
Doocot
Newark Castle

Starting Point: St Monans Church

Directions to start

A917 coast road from St Andrews or the B9131 to
Anstruther, where it joins the A917. At St Monans
go down Station Road and turn right into
Braehead. Follow this road and it leads directly to
the Church at the south west corner of the village.

Recommended Maps

Ordnance Survey Landranger 59
East Neuk & Largo Street Plan (2nd edition)

Distance: 1 mile
(can be extended by following the old railway
line to Elie, about 1 mile south west)

St Monans Old Church (1) is a massive structure of great antiquity standing right on the edge of the land. In places its churchyard wall falls away until there is nothing to stop you walking straight out over the small cliff into the sea. No church in Scotland is closer to the sea, and in a community as closely associated with the sea as this one, its position seems wholly appropriate.

The town of St Monans derives its name from **St Ninian**, Monan being the Gaelic version of Ninian, and the church has been a place of Christian worship for many centuries, serving as a place of pilgrimage, a shrine and a priory of the Dominican Order.

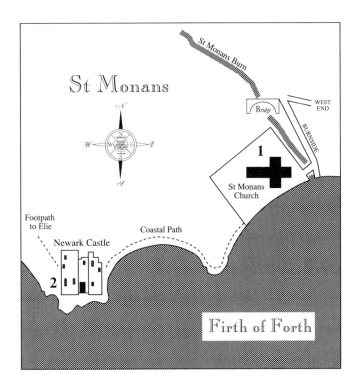

One legend suggests that the church may have become a Royal Chapel as early as the 12th century, as a result of **King David I** (1085-1153) being cured of an arrow wound by the monks of St Monans after the Battle of the Standard in 1138. But most of the building work took place in the 14th century during the reign of **David II**. In 1471 the church was given to the Dominican Order. In 1544 it was burned by the English, but no great damage was done. By the late 18th century the church had fallen into disrepair—J. G. Mackay described it as 'partly honeycombed by the weather and unroofed', although in the early 19th century it was restored by **William Burn**.

The exterior of the church is starkly medieval, its walls, choir, transepts and steeple having retained much of their original character despite all the restoration work done in the last 200 years. The

St Monans Church

choir windows, for example have survived from the middle ages and are not the 19th century replacements usually to be found in churches of this period. The interior of the church is very simple, the whole having been whitewashed fairly recently. A model boat hangs from the roof under the crossing, and in the north east end of the church there are information boards giving details of St Monans history.

One of these tells of the great disaster of the winter of 1875, when 5 boats and 37 men of St Monans and Cellardyke were lost in hurricane weather off the coast of Norfolk. The names of the boats were *Beautiful Star, Thane, Quest, Janet Anderson* and *Vigilant*. The wreck of *Beautiful Star* was discovered drifting off Kings Lynn eight days after the storm by the steam packet *Sea Nymph*:

> 'It was a mournful symbol of the cruel
> sea. The waves were washing over the
> gunwale of the fishing boat, as she
> proved to be. There was not a trace of the
> crew....the wreck was taken in tow, and
> eventually berthed at Lynn. The chances
> of salvage sent the men of the Sea Nymph
> quickly to work to bale their prize, now
> seen to be the "Beautiful Star". An
> entrance was made into the cabin, in the
> bow of the boat. Here a terrible discovery
> was made – five of the crew lying lifeless
> on the floor....All is conjecture, but the
> fact that Skipper James Paterson was
> severely cleft in the temple has induced
> many to believe that the others were
> giving the assistance or relief they could
> when their own fate was sealed by the
> swamping of the boat. But to the end they

were faithful to duty.'
George Gourlay
Memorials of Cellardyke (1879)

When the men of the *Beautiful Star* were buried in
Kings Lynn, over two hundred and fifty fishermen
and thousands of local people turned out.

Several families were virtually wiped out in this
disaster and **Sir Robert Anstruther** of Balcaskie and
his wife organised a relief fund for the dependants
of those who had lost their lives, writing to all the
newspapers of the day:

> 'Sir, I do not think I need apologise for
> asking some assistance from the public
> through your columns for the many
> amongst the fishing population in our
> immediate neighbourhood who have
> suffered from the late storms. We have
> lost two boats belonging to Cellardyke
> and three belonging to St Monans, with
> the whole of their crews; and the
> sorrow, misery and want in those
> towns are of a kind that I cannot
> attempt to describe. Such a catastrophe,
> under any circumstances sufficiently
> dreadful, is in these cases rendered still
> more calamitous by the fact that many
> of the boats crews are closely related to
> each other by family ties. In the town of
> St Monans, one unfortunate woman,
> Mrs Paterson, has lost at one blow her
> husband, her son, two brothers, three
> nephews, a brother-in-law and a
> cousin; another, Mrs Allan, about
> seventy years of age, has lost her two
> sons, her two nephews, her son-in-law,
> and two grandsons. A public meeting

will be convened by the Provost of Anstruther on Monday, the 6th day of December, in order to obtain aid for the sufferers...The above two small towns have lost at one blow 37 of the flower of their sea-going man, 19 women are left widows; and 72 children are made orphans, besides, several aged persons dependent upon the deceased men have been deprived of their support.

I am, &c,

Robert Anstruther'

£7,206:15s/3d was raised and distributed amongst the bereaved at the rate of 4s a week to each widow, 1s 6d a week to each child under 15, and 3s a week to other dependants.

On leaving the church you may notice a ships porthole set into the door. The churchyard has steps that lead right onto the shoreline. Go down these steps and follow the line of the churchyard wall back towards the west until it joins the coastal path that leads to Newark Castle.

Before you reach the castle you go past the 16th century doocot on the cliffs. Traditional beehive doocots like this one are to be found throughout Fife and the Lothians, and they were used to house pigeons as a source of fresh meat in the winter.

*Continue on to the ruins of **Newark Castle (2)**.*

Newark Castle, or St Monans Castle as it was originally known, probably dates from the 15th century, although much of what now remains is of a later date. The castle passed through the hands of several local families until it was sold by Lord Abercrombie in 1649 to **General Sir David Leslie**.

Leslie had fought for **Gustavus Adolphus** in the Thirty Years War and returned to fight as a general with the Covenanters against Charles I. At the **Battle of Marston Moor** in 1644 he played a major part in Cromwell's victory. Recalled to Scotland to fight against Montrose, he ended Montrose's year of victories by defeating him at **Philiphaugh** in the Borders on 13th September 1645. This battle became infamous as a result of the massacre of Montrose's Irish troops by Leslie's men: they were herded into the courtyard of **Newark Castle** near Selkirk and shot along with their camp followers. This action earned Leslie the nickname 'The Executioner'. By 1650, in a turnaround typical of the convoluted politics of the time, Leslie had taken Charles II's side and was in command of the Covenanting army *against* Cromwell at the Battle of Dunbar. He was defeated and, after being captured the following year at the Battle of Worcester, spent the rest of the decade as a prisoner in the Tower of London.

On the restoration of **Charles II**, Leslie was created Lord Newark in 1661, rather ironic in view of his involvement in the massacre at that other Newark. He also received a pension of £500 a year, although not everyone shared the King's high opinion of Leslie—one courtier remarked at the time, that he ought rather to have been brought to the gallows for his 'auld wark'.

It was about this time that Leslie set about extending and improving the castle. The north east part of the main block of the castle still shows traces of the work he carried out, particularly in the elegant, though fragmentary, curvilinear gable end. Apart from this, the most substantial parts of the castle now standing are a series of vaulted cellars in the

Newark Castle

block facing the sea and these date from the earliest phase of the castle's construction. Although the castle is now very much a crumbling ruin, it has apparently only fallen into this state in the last hundred years and it seems rather sad that no one took the trouble to preserve what must once have been one of Scotland's most dramatically sited castles.

From Newark Castle there are two options: either return along the coastal path (or along the beach at low tide) to St Monans; or head west along the coastal path to Elie and Earlsferry.

14

ELIE

<u>THE TOWN AND THE BEACH</u>

Parish Church
High Street
The Toft
Sea Wall & Harbour
Coastal Walk
Lighthouse
Lady's Tower
Ruby Bay

Staring Point: Elie Parish Church

Directions to Start
B9131 south from St Andrews,
then A917 south west to Elie

Recommended Maps:
Ordnance Survey Landranger 59
East Neuk & Largo Street Plan (2nd edition)

Distance: 2 miles

Elie went through a period of decline in the 18th century until its popularity as a seaside resort gave it a new lease of life in the Victorian era. This walk begins in the centre of the town outside the **Parish Church (1)**.

This church was built by **Sir William Scott of Ardross** and was completed in 1639. The tower is a later addition, and was built by **Sir John Anstruther** in 1726. His contribution to the church is commemorated in the inscription over the door.

Leaving the church, turn eastwards along the High Street, and turn right into Stenton Road. This road leads onto The Toft and past The Ship Inn. Continue round to the harbour.

The development of the harbour began in the late 16th century, the pier itself being renovated in the middle of the 19th century. In 1715 the **Earl of Mar** landed here on his way to take part in the Jacobite rising of that year. On the harbour wall itself you will see a three storeyed building which used to be a granary. From the harbour wall adjoining the granary there is an excellent view across to Earlsferry. During the summer, dinghies, windsurfers and canoes can be hired at the harbour. (Tel: 0333 310366)

Head back the way you have just come and turn right up the first road you come to. This takes you across the top of Ruby Bay—so called because small semi-precious stones have apparently been found in the sand there—to the car park which is the start of the coastal walk. From the car park you will see the lighthouse to the south. Walk down to the lighthouse, crossing the small bridge.

This lighthouse, which dates from 1908, is not particularly old or unusual, but it is beautifully situated on the promontory and commands delightful views of the East Lothian coastline.

*From the lighthouse return across the small bridge and follow the line of the coast eastwards along to the **Lady's Tower.***

This ruined tower was originally constructed as an elaborate bathing hut for **Lady Janet Fall** of Elie House. There is also a small cave in the cliffs beneath the Lady's Tower that is worth a look.

Continue past the tower and follow the coast northwards before turning west and heading back to the car park above Ruby Bay.

Elie Harbour

15

EARLSFERRY

THE CHAIN WALK

Chapel Green
West Bay
Caves
Shell Bay
Grangehill

Starting Point: Chapel Green

Directions to Start
B9131 south from St Andrews,
then A917 south west to Earlsferry

Recommended Maps
Ordnance Survey Landranger 59
East Neuk & Largo Street Plan (2nd edition)

Distance: 3 miles

Warning: In places this is a demanding walk,
involving a certain amount of scrambling and
climbing, especially at high tide, so you will need
a good pair of boots. Take a torch if you want to
look around the caves.

West Bay

Starting at **Chapel Ness**, head west to the start of the chain walk at the far side of the West Bay. This walk is not an easy one and some sections are more or less impassable at high tide. It is advisable to check the tides with the coastguard (Tel: 0333 50293) before setting out, and allow a couple of hours to reach Shell Bay (although it shouldn't take that long). On the more difficult sections look out for the steps that have been worn in the rock outcrops and the chains that mark the only route over the more impassable obstacles. The first chains are at **Kincraig Point**.

> *From **Chapel Green** follow the path that leads onto the coast, just past the fragmentary ruins of an old chapel at **Chapel Ness**.*

In the 1850's a number of stone coffins were discovered close to the shore and these were believed to contain the remains of Viking raiders killed in battle close to Earlsferry some time around 1033. The chapel may have been a hospice run by **Cistercian nuns**, one of whose functions was to keep lamps burning as an early form of lighthouse to aid those crossing the Forth.

*The path then skirts round the golf course, but if the tide is out head straight across the sands of the **West Bay** to **Kincraig Point**, clearly visible as the rocky outcrop on the other side of the bay.*

Around Kincraig Point you will come across a number of caves, one of which is said to have been the refuge of **Macduff**, the Thane of Fife, while he was being pursued by Macbeth. It is from this incident, and Macduff's subsequent escape by ferry, that Earlsferry got its name. Two other caves at this point are known as **Doo Cave** and **The Devils Cave**. From here onwards the walk becomes quite tricky in places as the chains appear. Some of the rock formations that the chains help you across are very dramatic indeed and great care should be taken in negotiating them.

It is not possible to give exact directions, you must simply follow the steps and the chains wherever possible and avoid any patches of rock that look particularly treacherous. At the mouth of the largest cave there seems no choice but to leap across a gully, but if you head right up to the cave you should be able to get across more easily and traverse back to the next chain.

Although rugged at times, the scenery around **Kincraig Point**, with its stony beaches and tower-

The Chain Walk

ing cliffs, easily outweighs the perils of scrambling up and down 20 foot drops while loosely attached to an antique chain.

*Once around Kincraig Point you come to the sandy beach of **Shell Bay**. Follow the coastal path around the edge of the fields until you reach Shell Bay Caravan Park. From here follow the road out of the caravan park before turning right at the point where the road forks, and a little way up this road take the lane that goes off to the left to Grangehill. Follow this lane through the houses, past the ruined **Grange**.*

The Grange was originally the site of a convent of the nuns of North Berwick, who first came here at the end of the 12th century. They remained in possession of the Grange until 1560, when they sold it for £1000 to **Alexander Wood**, Minister of Largo, and son of Admiral Wood of Largo. The ruins that can be seen today are probably those of a house built on this site by **James Malcolm**, who bought the estate in 1708. A prominent Jacobite who fought and was captured at the Battle of Killiecrankie, Malcolm had the house designed specifically for ease of defence.

*Continue down onto the path across the golf course. From here turn right and head back to **Chapel Green**.*

16

UPPER LARGO TO LOWER LARGO

Largo Parish Church
Largo House
Sir Andrew Wood's Tower
'The Canal'
Serpentine Walk
Alexander Selkirk
Coastal Walk

Starting Point: **Largo Parish Church**

Directions to Start
Follow the A915 south west from St Andrews,
passing through Largoward to Upper Largo.

Recommended Map
Ordnance Survey Landranger 59

Distance: 3 miles

Tearoom: Upper Largo Hotel

Largo Parish Church (1) is beautifully situated high above Upper Largo. The first church to stand here was consecrated by Bishop David de Bernham in July 1243; although most of the present building is much more modern: the nave and transepts were built in 1816-17, and the chancel, tower and steeple date from the 1620's.

A number of steps lead into the churchyard and immediately to the right of the steps is an ancient **Pictish Stone**. The carving on the stone is now badly worn away, but is said to depict a cross with seahorses on one side, and three horsemen and an elephant on the other side. It was found in 1839, broken in two and being used as a drain cover. **General James Durham** had it restored and erected in the grounds of Largo House. It moved with the Durham family to Polton House, but was eventually returned to Largo and set up in its present position.

General Durham was also involved in an earlier discovery when, in 1819, a labourer working on Norrie's Law (part of Largo Law, the hill behind the village) unearthed a stone coffin containing an ancient suit of chain mail armour, along with other weapons and items of silver jewellery. Durham acquired some of these items and they were eventually put on display in the Royal Museum of Scotland in Edinburgh.

> *Follow the path around to the right of the church and just past the bench you will come to an unusual 18th century tombstone.*

This commemorates the deaths of the children of **John Fortune**, two of whom died within a day of each other and were buried in the same coffin. On the other side of the stone there are the figures of a man and a woman—no doubt John Fortune and his wife.

Close to the path in the north west corner of the churchyard is a stone marked with the initials JS and EM. This is the grave of John Selkirk and Euphan Mackie, who were the parents of Alexander Selkirk. It was a family dispute with his parents and his brothers that led Alexander Selkirk to set out on the adventures that were later immortalised in the novel *Robinson Crusoe*.

Follow the path back around to the main door of the church.

The interior of the church contains an impressive wooden hammerbeam roof, plus a number of 19th century plaques and monuments commemorating local dignitaries such as **Admiral Sir Philip Charles Henderson Calderwood Durham** (1763-1845), whose family owned the mansion just to the west of the church and who 'Passed his latter years chiefly at Fordel, courted in society and generously spending an ample fortune'.

As a young man Philip Durham was serving as a Lieutenant on the *Royal George* when it sank off Spithead. He was the first to notice that the ship was listing to starboard, and had just managed to call out 'The ship is sinking!' when it suddenly capsized. Durham escaped through a porthole, but was nearly drowned when a marine seized his jacket and they both began to sink. Durham managed to throw off his jacket and the unfortunate marine, whose body was found several days later still grasping Durham's jacket. Only 70 out of a crew of 1200 survived. A gun taken from the wreck used to stand in front of Largo House. Durham was later mentioned-in-dispatches for his bravery at Trafalgar in 1805, and was involved in the capture of Guadaloupe in 1815.

Another member of the family, **James Durham**, was a noted golfer whose score of 94 on the Old Course at St Andrews in 1767 remained unbeaten for almost 100 years.

The 1914-18 War Memorial on the south wall of the nave includes the names of four members of the same family—the Anderson brothers from Strathairly, one of whom, Colonel W. H. Anderson, was awarded a posthumous Victoria Cross.

Just to the left of the door, at the west end of the church, is a poignant memorial to Richard Muckersie 'boy 1st Class, RN, lost overboard from *HMS Dunedin*, 10th Sept 1939 on active service.'

On leaving the church, you will see a plaque set in the outside of the churchyard wall to the right of the gate. This commemorates the building of the wall in 1657 by **John Wood**.

A.D.1657

AFTER 55 YEARS ABSENCE RETURNING FROM
HIS TRAVELS CAUSED BUILD THIS WALL
ABOUT THIS CHURCHYARD IN MEMORY
THAT HIS PREDECESSORS AND HIS PARENTS
LYES BURIED IN LARGO IYLLE
JOHN WOOD ESQUIRE

When John Wood died in Edinburgh in February 1661, he left instructions that he was to be buried in the family vault in Largo Church; but as the result of a Dickensian dispute over his legitimacy and his will, his body lay unburied in Elie Church until the 22nd July, when he was finally laid to rest as he had wished.

Continue straight ahead down East Drive until you come to a gate. Just beyond this in the clump of trees to the left are the ruins of Largo House (2).

Largo House was built in 1750 for the **Durham family** who bought the estate from Sir Alexander Gibson of Durie in the 1660's. The Durham's were descendants of **Sir William Durham of Grange** who had been a prominent noble at the time of Robert the Bruce. Sir Alexander Durham was Lord Lyon King of Arms in 1660. The family eventually sold the estate in 1868.

Even in its present ruinous state the house retains a sense of its 18th century grandeur, although to look at it it hardly seems possible that it was still occupied at least until the mid 1930's.

The pedimented Georgian doorway bears many of

Largo House

the hallmarks of the work of the Adam family, and the diagonal dressing of the stonework is similar to that to be seen in the work of **John Adam**. Looking above the doorway, it is still possible to read the family motto: 'Victoria Non Praede, Per Mare Per Terras' and the date 1750. Just around to the north side of the house are the remains of the 19th century stables, picturesquely overgrown with ivy and now serving as a shelter for cattle.

> Go back to the wall at the end of East Drive and follow it towards the ruined stable block behind Largo House. Just to the right there is a gateway through into the field in front of the garden wall of **Old Largo House (3)**. Cross the field to the gap in the wall on the other side, go through this gap, and turn left to the ruins of Wood's Tower.

Not much is left of **Old Largo House,** only the tower, known as **Sir Andrew Wood's Tower,** is still standing. This is the late 16th or early 17th century corner tower of a house that was originally built for Sir Andrew Wood in the late 15th century.

Sir Andrew Wood (1460-1540) was a prominent Scottish seafarer, who served both James III and IV and defeated the English in a number of naval engagements in the Firth of Forth in 1489-90.

One of his most celebrated victories was against five English ships sent by **Henry VII** to pillage the fishing villages of the Forth. Wood's ships *The Flower* and *The Yellow Caravel* (a model of which can be seen in the Nave of Largo Church) met the English off Dunbar and defeated them, capturing all five of their vessels. This moved Henry VII to offer £1000 to anyone who could defeat Wood and bring him to London, dead or alive. An English seafarer, **Stephen Bull**, took up the challenge and attacked Wood with three ships close to the Isle of May in July 1490. After a battle lasting two days, Wood was victorious once more. After presenting Bull and his other prisoners at King James' Court, Wood chivalrously allowed them to return to England.

Admiral Wood was knighted by **James III** in 1482 and given the lands and village of Largo in recognition of his services to the Crown. In his later years, when he could no longer go to sea, Sir Andrew had the rather unusual idea of having a canal dug between his house and the church a few hundred yards to the east. This was done so that he could be taken to church in a barge. The faint remains of the line of this unique venture can still just about be seen to the north east of the tower running towards the church. Admiral Wood was buried under the aisle of Largo Church.

> *Return to the church and head up Church Place to Main Street, turn right, walk past the garage on your right, and head down the main road till you reach the start of the **Serpentine Walk (4)**. On the way you will see a house on your left, at the start of South Feus, which has an unusual curved gable end with an owl on top.*

The Serpentine Walk is a pleasant woodland walk that begins close to the impressive old gateway to Largo House. It leads down to Lower Largo, emerging on the line of the old coastal railway. Before the path reaches Lower Largo there are a couple of benches from which, on a clear day, there are good views of the Firth of Forth, the coast of East Lothian, Bass Rock, Arthur's Seat and the Hopetoun Monument.

> *From the end of the Serpentine Walk, turn right and walk along Main Street until you come to the **Alexander Selkirk Memorial (5)** of 1885 in a niche above the door of the house that stands on the site of his birthplace.*

Alexander Selkirk (1681-1728) was the sailor whose adventures formed the basis of Daniel Defoe's novel ***'Robinson Crusoe'***. Selkirk, who originally went to sea to escape legal proceedings over a fight with his father and his brother and his 'undecent beavier in ye church', was the master of the privateer *Cinque Ports* and 'the best man on her', when a quarrel with the Captain led to him being marooned on the island of **Mas a Tierra,** one of three uninhabited islands in the Juan Fernandez group, 400 miles off the Chilean coast. He was to remain there for almost four and a half years, until he was rescued by the privateer *Duke* in February 1709. Selkirk told **Captain Rogers** of the *Duke*:

'that he was born in Scotland and was bred a sailor from his youth....he had

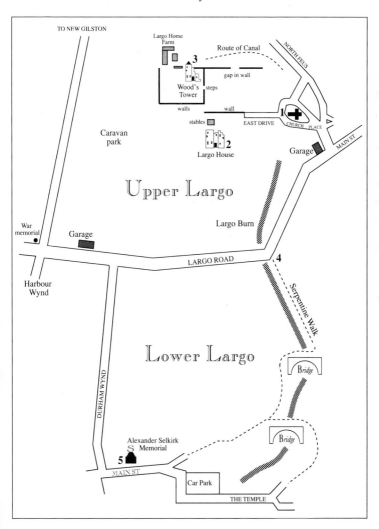

with him his clothes and bedding, with
a firelock, some powder, bullets, and
tobacco, a hatchet, a knife, a bible, some
practical pieces, and his mathematical
instruments and books. He diverted
and provided for himself as well as he
could, but for the first eight months
had much ado to bear up against
melancholy.'

The story of Robinson Crusoe was published in
1719 under the title *The Life and Strange Surprizing
Adventures of Robinson Crusoe of York, Mariner*. The
novel deals with the predicament of a sailor who is
marooned on a deserted tropical island, 'Having
been cast on shore by shipwreck, wherin all the men
perished but himself':

'I now began to consider seriously my
condition, and the circumstance I was
reduced to, and I drew up the state of
my affairs in writing, not so much to
leave them to any that were to come
after me, for I was like to have but few
heirs, as to deliver my thoughts from
daily poring upon them, and afflicting
my mind; and as my reason began now
to master my despondency, I began to
comfort my self as well as I could, and
to set the good against the evil, that I
might have something to distinguish
my case from worse, and I stated it
very impartially, like debtor and
creditor, the comforts I enjoyed against
the miseries I suffered, thus:

Evil	*Good*
I am cast upon a horrible desolate island, void of all hope of recovery.	But I am alive, and not drowned as all my ship's company was.
I am singled out and separated, as it were, from all the world to be miserable.	But I am singled out too from all the ship's crew to be spared from death; and he that miraculously saved me from death can deliver me from this condition.
I am divided from mankind, a solitaire, one banished from humane society.	But I am not starved and perishing on a barren place, affording no sustenance.
I have not clothes to cover me.	But I am in a hot climate, where if I had clothes I could hardly wear them.
I am without any defence or means to resist any violence of man or beast.	But I am cast on an island, where I see no wild beasts to hurt me, as I saw on the coast of Africa; and what if I had been shipwrecked there?
I have no soul to speak to, or relieve me.	But God wonderfully sent the ship in near enough to the shore that I have gotten out so many necessary things as will either supply my wants or enable me to supply my self even as long as I live.

Upon the whole, here was an undoubted testimony, that there was scarce any condition in the world so miserable, but that there was something negative or something positive to be thankful for in it; and let this stand as a direction from the experience of the most miserable of all conditions in this world, that we may always find in it something to comfort ourselves from.'

Daniel Defoe
The Life and Adventures of
Robinson Crusoe

Captain Rogers took Selkirk on as mate of the *Duke*, and he eventually returned home with £800 in prize money. On his return to Britain, Selkirk met **Daniel Defoe** and told him his story—which Defoe promptly turned into one of the world's best known novels.

After living near Largo on Balcarres Craig 'because he could not stand the sound of the human voice', Selkirk returned to sea and died of yellow fever aged 47 while serving as a Lieutenant on board *HMS Weymouth* off the coast of West Africa in 1728.

From here either return to the start via the Serpentine Walk, or turn right into Durham Wynd and then right where it joins the Largo Road, following this road back to the start of the walk.

17

EARLSHALL CASTLE AND LEUCHARS

Earlshall Castle
Gardens
Leuchars Village
St Athernase Church
Churchyard

Starting Point: Earlshall Castle

Directions to Start
A91 to Guardbridge, then A919 to Leuchars

Opening Times
Earlshall Castle: Summer 2-6pm,
Closed during the winter.

Recommended Map
Ordnance Survey Landranger 59

Distance: 4 miles

Tearoom
Earlshall Castle

Earlshall Castle (1) was begun by **Sir William Bruce** in 1546 and completed by his great grandson in 1617. A fine example of a 16th century tower house, it has survived remarkably intact, the only major restoration work having been done by **Robert Lorimer** in the 1890's. When Earlshall was purchased in 1890 by **Robert MacKenzie**, a Dundee merchant, he wisely chose Lorimer to undertake its restoration. It was Lorimer's first commission—he was only 26—but the work he carried out preserved and enhanced the house without destroying its original character. Lorimer was also responsible for the restoration of the gardens in a traditional Scottish style.

Inside the house the two most significant rooms are the Great Hall and the Long Gallery. **The Great Hall** is panelled in oak and the walls are hung with a wide variety of antique weapons—ranging from an unusual French six-shot flintlock rifle of the late 17th century, to the standard arms of the clansman: the broadsword and targe. There is also a child's suit of armour and a selection of evil-looking crossbows. Before Lorimer's time this room and the dining room had been divided by an 18th century partition wall and he replaced this with an oak screen modelled on the rood screen at **Falkland Palace**. It carries the inscription:

TAK TIME IN TIME ERE TIME BE TINT
FOR TIME WILL NO REMAIN AD 1891

The Long Gallery is over fifty feet long and occupies the whole of the second floor of the main block. It was largely the work of the second Sir William Bruce and his wife Agnes Lindsay in the early years of the 17th century. The wooden vaulted ceiling is decorated in tempera with the coats of arms of the major families of Scotland and Europe and depictions of mythical animals after Conrad Gesner's *Historia Animalium* of 1551. The painted arcading along the walls contains a number of aphorisms, the best of which is to the left of the door as you go in:

A NICE WYF AND A BACK DOORE
OFT MAKETH A RICH MAN POORE

The whitewashed walls of the gallery are lined with the present owner's extensive collection of swords, dating from 1550 to 1800. At both ends of the Long Gallery there are large mural paintings of dogs—at the western end Robert Mackenzie's bloodhound 'Earl' by David Steell (1895) with an inscription taken from Byron; and at the eastern end Major Baxter's golden retriever 'George' by Kenneth Johnson.

The Garden at Earlshall is very impressive, with its yew topiary laid out in the shape of four Saltires. The trees originally came from an old garden in Edinburgh and cost £5 each. Lorimer intended the garden to be closely related to the house—he apparently disliked the vast rolling parklands attached to many Baronial style houses. Lorimer obviously had a sense of humour as well, as can be seen in the stone monkeys climbing up the Garden House in the north west corner and on the roof of the Garden Store. In the east wall there is a fine gateway with this inscription:

HERE SHALL YE SEE NO ENEMY BVT
WINTER AND ROVGH WEATHER

On leaving the castle, turn left and there is a short

woodland walk that leads south west past a 17th century Doocot back to the car park. From here follow the track back to the road, turn left and follow the road to Leuchars village. Across the first junction you come to is **Leuchars Parish Church.**

St Athernase Church is a most unusual looking building on a small hill dominating the village of Leuchars. Built some time before 1185, it is one of the finest examples of a Norman church to be seen in Britain. Originally, it was granted to the Priory of St Andrews by **Nes, Lord of Lochore** (Leuchars) around 1187; although the de Quinci family, who rebuilt Leuchars Castle in the 12th century, took over the patronage of the church in the early years of the 13th century. It was not until 1244 that **Bishop David de Bernham** of St Andrews dedicated the church to St Athernase—an Irish saint who may have been a contemporary of **St Columba**.

It seems likely that the church was built by the same masons who worked on **Dalmeny Church** in West Lothian, another fine example of Romanesque architecture, as identical mason's marks can be seen at both churches. At St Athernase these marks can be seen on stones in the Chancel and the Apse.

Although the church has been greatly altered over the years, much of the original Norman work survives—externally the two tiers of blind arcading around the Apse and Choir, and the corbels elaborately carved with gargoyles and animals are most impressive; while the interior of the church retains intact the fine carving on the arches of the Apse and Chancel. The main change to the church came with the building of the belltower sometime between 1660 and 1700. This octagonal tower with its stone

St Athernase

lantern on top has been much criticised on the basis
that it spoils the Norman lines of the original
building, but many would argue that with its
weathered appearance it blends in well with the
original. Attempts to have it pulled down during
the restorations of 1857-8 and 1914 both failed on
the grounds of cost.

Inside the church there are a number of interesting
memorials, in particular those of the Bruce family
who lived at Earlshall Castle. A memorial stone
mounted beside the south door commemorates **Sir
William Bruce**, who fought at Flodden in 1513,
built Earlshall and died there in 1584 aged 98.

HIC IACET VIR PROBUS AC OMNI METIOMRIA
DIGNUS DNS GUILLIELMUS BRYCEUS DE

ERLISHAL MILES OBIIT 28 DIE MENSIS IANVARII
ANNO DNI 1584 ANNOQUE SUEATATIS 98
MORS OMNIUM EST FINIS W.B.
BE TREW

which translates as: 'Here lies an upright man and
worthy to be held in remembrance of all Sir William
Bruce of Earlshall Knight who died 28th January
1584 in the 98th year of his age Death is the end of
all'. Beneath this is the following inscription:

HEIR LIES OF ALL PIETE ANE LANTERNE BRYCHT
SCHIR VILLIAM BRVCE OF ERLISHALL NYCHT

On the other side of the doorway is the memorial to
Agnes Lindsay, second wife of the great grandson
of Sir William Bruce:

D. AGNES LINDSAY LADY TO WILLIAM BRUCE
OF ERLSHALL WHO IN HER LIFE WAS
CHARITABLE TO THE POORE AND PROFITABLE
TO THAT HOUSE DYED 1635
OF HER AGE 68 AND
WAITETH HERE IN HOPE

Set in the floor near the pulpit is the memorial to Sir
Robert Carnegy who died in 1565. His family at one
time owned Leuchars Castle.

UNDER THIS STONE LIES THE BODY
OF THE WORTHY SIR ROBERT CARNEGY
OF KINNAIRD, LORD OF SESSION,
WHO DIED IN THE CASTLE OF LEUCHARS
5TH JANUARY 1565 AGED 55

On leaving the church it is worth having a look
around the churchyard. Close to the wall of the
church on the north side is the grave of John Finch,

master mariner of Maldon in Essex who was drowned with five others in St Andrews Bay on 28th January 1848:

> 'The name of the Lord is a strong tower.
> The righteous runneth into it and is safe.'
> ***Proverbs***

Another interesting gravestone is that of William Taylor, a local shoemaker who died in 1835, which has the traditional tools of his trade carved upon it.

The churchyard marks the end of the walk.

18

FALKLAND

Falkland Palace
Moncrief House
Parish Church
Bruce Fountain
Cameron's House
Reading Room
Old Burial Ground

Starting Point: Falkland Palace

Directions to Start
A91 to Cupar, then A92 to the roundabout,
then A912 to Falkland

Opening Times
Falkland Palace: summer 10am-6pm
Sunday afternoons only.
Closed during the winter.

Recommended Map
Ordnance Survey Landranger 59

Distance: 1 to 2 miles

Tearoom
Hayloft, Back Wynd

Falkland Palace (1) stands on the site of an earlier castle, which was razed to the ground by the army of Edward III in 1337, rebuilt by the start of the 15th century, and finally disappeared around 1610—by which time it had been replaced by the Royal Palace. At one time the castle had been garrisoned by more than 200 men.

The new palace was begun by **James IV** in 1501; although **James II** had begun to convert the old castle into something more suitable as a Royal residence in the 1450's. The palace was intended to serve as a Royal hunting lodge, and the forest of Falkland was specially protected for this purpose at a time when the other woods of Fife were being felled for ship-building. **James V** is even said to have imported wild boar from the continent to add to the local wildlife.

After 1537, it was James V who began the work of turning Falkland into a renaissance palace. All the Stewart Kings either lived at Falkland or visited regularly—**James V** died there in 1542, **Mary Queen of Scots** played real tennis there, **Charles I** visited in 1633, and **Charles II** stayed there briefly in 1651 while staking his claim to the Scottish throne.

In 1654, when Cromwell's troops were billeted here, a disastrous fire destroyed part of the palace. From then onwards, due to the neglect of a series of Hereditary Keepers, the palace fell into decline, and by the early years of the 19th century it was sadly decayed—partly unroofed and boarded up. In this state it passed through many hands until **John Crichton Stuart, 3rd Marquess of Bute** bought the title of Hereditary Keeper in 1887 and set about its restoration. He was largely responsible for bringing what had once been a forgotten and dilapidated ruin back to the condition in which it stands today. His grandson, **Major Michael Crichton Stuart** made the National Trust for Scotland Deputy Keeper in 1952.

The most striking external feature of the palace is the massive south western **Gatehouse**. This was the last part of the palace to be finished, just before James V died in 1542. Adjoining the gatehouse is the south range which houses the **Royal Chapel**. On the front of the gatehouse you will see the brightly painted coat of arms of the Marquess of Bute, placed here during the restoration work of the 1890's.

From the entrance in the gatehouse you pass into the entrance hall, and from here you will be escorted on a guided tour by one of the National Trust Guides.

In the **South Range** you pass through the Keeper's bedroom, with its ornate four poster bed that is reputed to have belonged to **James VI**, the dressing room, and the drawing room with its double portrait of James V and Mary of Lorraine over the fireplace. A door leads directly from the drawing room into the **Royal Chapel**.

On the wall just to the left of the oak entrance screen there is a fine icon of Our Lady of Ostrobrama which was made out of brass shell cases and corned beef tins by Polish paratroops stationed here during the Second World War. The Chapel itself dates from James V's time and is well lit due to its large south facing windows. The 17th century tapestries on the north wall are Flemish, and the ancient looking pulpit may be the original 16th century one.

The East Range

From the Chapel you pass along the **Tapestry Gallery**, hung with more 17th century Flemish tapestries depicting animals and hunting scenes, to the **Old Library**, with its elaborate ceiling and collection of Crichton Stuart memorabilia.

The tour then heads out onto the **East Range**, roofless as a result of the fire in 1654. In the centre of the east range is the **Cross House** which was restored by the Marquess of Bute. The two rooms in the Cross House have been restored to give an idea of what Royal State bedrooms would have looked like in the 16th century, even though this is not where they were situated in the palace.

The King's bedroom is equipped with the extremely ornate Golden Bed of Brahan, dating from the time of James VI. The walls and ceiling have been painted in a rather garish style which is said to be typical of the time. The heraldic device over the fireplace looks particularly incongruous.

*The turnpike stair leads up to the **Queen's Room**.*

The effect of the oak vaulted ceiling of this room is very impressive, and the cabinet beside the bed is said to be a replica of one that belonged to Archbishop Sharp.

From this room the turnpike stair leads to the garden.

The palace garden was designed just after the Second World War by Percy Cane, who had landscaped the garden of Haile Selassie in Addis Ababa. At the far end of the garden is the **Royal Tennis Court**. This was built in 1539 for James V and is the oldest such court in Britain. The game played here is very different from lawn tennis, and there are very few courts in the world where this version can be played. One other was built at Hampton Court in the 17th century.

Return through the garden to the courtyard of the palace.

From the Courtyard the damage done by the fire of 1654 can be clearly seen. Of the **East Range** only the facade and the cellars are more or less intact. By contrast, the **South Range** retains the elegant facade it was given in the time of **James V**. The five bay ashlar facade is decorated with laurel wreaths, carved heads and elaborate buttresses that were probably the work of the French mason, **Nicolas Roy**.

Leave the palace and walk up the High Street.

Directly opposite the palace is **Moncrief House (2)**.
This impressive thatched house dates from 1610,
when it was built for one of James VI's courtiers,
Nicol Moncrief. Just below a first floor window you
can still see this inscription, picked out in gold:

AL PRAISE TO GOD AND THANKIS TO
THE MOST EXCELLENT MONARCHE GREAT
BRITANE OF WHOSE PRINCELIE LIBERALITIE
THIS IS MY PORTIOVNE DEO LAVS ESTO FIDVS
ADEST MERCES NICOLL MONCRIEF
1610

Next door in the wall of the Falkland Arms there are
two further inscriptions, one marked 'BW 1607',
with the motto 'contentment is great riches', and
another from the reign of James VI:

I.R.6 GOD SAIF YE KING OF GREAT BRITAN
FRANCE AND IRLAND OVR SOVERAN FOR OF
HIS LIBERALITY THIS HOVS DID I EDIFY

Continue west along the High Street and on the left
you pass the Bank of Scotland, formerly the **British
Linen Bank (3)**—a reminder of the days when
Falkland was a centre of the hand loom weaving
industry.

Opposite the bank are three houses, the two outer
ones are 18th century and have appropriate marriage lintels—one dated 1777. The house in the
centre, now a gift shop, was once the home of **Sir
George Deas (4)**, a 19th century Lord of Session,
and its more ornate facade reflects his position in
society.

Cross Back Wynd and you come to the **Town Hall (5)** built between 1800 and 1801. This building is now in the care of the National Trust and houses a variety of exhibits relating to the history of Falkland.

*Across the square is **Falkland Parish Church (6)**.*

This church was built in 1848-50 on the site of a 17th century church. **David Bryce** was the architect, and the building was paid for by **Onesiphorus Tyndall Bruce** and his wife **Margaret** who built the House of Falkland and lived there from 1844.

Onesiphorus Tyndall Bruce, whose statue by **Sir John Steell** stands beside the church, was an English barrister. He came to Falkland when he married **Margaret Bruce**, who had inherited the lands of Falkland from her father, Professor John Bruce. Onesiphorus died in 1855, only 11 years after the House of Falkland was completed, and Margaret died in 1869. **The Bruce Fountain (7)** in the centre of the square, with its lions, shields and gothic spire, is a memorial to them.

*From the Bruce Fountain, cross the street and on south side of the square you will see two houses with crowstepped gables. **Cameron House (8)** has a plaque on the front marking it as the birthplace of **Richard Cameron**, the 'Lion of the Covenant'.*

Richard Cameron (1648-1680) was the son of a merchant and became a schoolmaster in Falkland, before being converted to the Presbyterian cause by field preachers. He joined the covenanters in the west of Scotland in opposition to Charles II, who they believed had perjured himself by breaking the

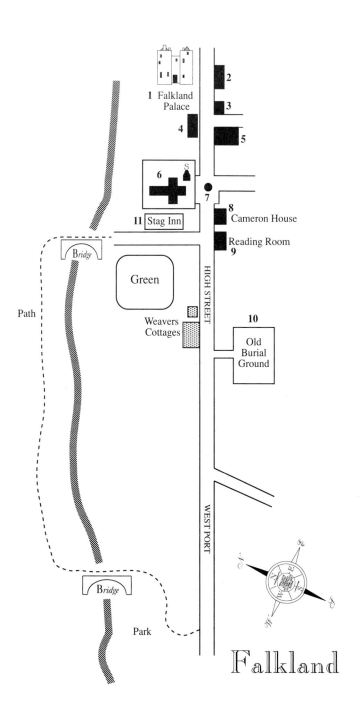

1 Falkland Palace

2

3

4

5

6

S

7

8 Cameron House

9 Reading Room

11 Stag Inn

10

Old Burial Ground

Bridge

Green

Path

Weavers Cottages

HIGH STREET

WEST PORT

Bridge

Park

Falkland

Covenant, and whose authority they would not therefore accept. Before the **Battle of Airdsmoss** in 1680, Cameron is said to have washed his hands more carefully than usual saying, 'It was need to make them clean, for there are many to see them'. During the battle he was killed, and his head and hands were cut off by **Sir Andrew Bruce of Earlshall**, 'that wicked and violent persecutor', who took them to Edinburgh where they were displayed on the Netherbow gate.

Continue west along from Cameron House to the junction with Mill Wynd and Rotten Row.

On the left is the **Old Reading Room (9)**. In the early part of the 18th century a family of 13 lived in the small upper flat, and in the 1850's the lower floor was used as a reading room, where newspapers and pamphlets were read aloud to local people. In the 1960's the house was converted into an electricity sub-station.

*Continue along the High Street, past the village green and the weavers cottages on the right, until you reach the **Old Burial Ground (10)** which is through a classical gateway on the left.*

The Old Burial Ground was used from the late 17th century onwards, and contains a number of 17th and 18th century tombstones, with the usual symbols of mortality—winged angels, angels sitting on skulls and hourglasses resting on skulls. Many of the inscriptions are too decayed to read, although one particularly morbid example has survived:

O LOOK AT ME AS YE PAS BY
AND BEAR ON MIND YOU HAVE TO DIE

*Leave the burial ground, turn left and continue along High Street to **West Port**. Go down West Port and turn right into the park, just after Hope Cottage. Follow the path through the park and alongside the **Maspie Burn** back towards the centre of the village. Cross the bridge at the foot of Mill Wynd and head up past the **Stag Inn (11)** (with its 17th century marriage lintel), back onto the High Street, and from there return to the start of the walk.*

19

EAST LOMOND AND WEST LOMOND

Lime Kilns
Hill Fort
East Lomond
Maiden Castle
West Lomond

Starting Point: Craigmead Car Park

Directions to Start
A91 to Cupar, then A92 to the roundabout, and
A912 to Falkland. Go through the centre of the
town and follow the sign for Craigmead Car
Park, about 1 mile outside Falkland.

Recommended Maps
Ordnance Survey Landranger 58 & 59

Distance
$1\frac{1}{4}$ miles to East Lomond
$2\frac{1}{2}$ miles to West Lomond

*From the **car park (1)** cross the road and follow the path across the hill towards **East Lomond**. Just below the point where the hill begins to steepen, another path heads off to the right. This leads to the **limekilns (2)** and the remains of the 19th century quarry.*

Limestone was quarried here in the 19th century and was mixed with coal before being fed into the limekilns that still stand here today. This process reduced the limestone to ash, which could then be used as an agricultural fertiliser. The actual work of feeding these giant furnaces was extremely hard—in the 1830's six men usually worked as a team and shifted about 2 tons of limestone per day. The working day lasted from 4am to 5pm, for which each man was paid ten shillings a week, which was less than half what a miner was paid at that time.

Lime Kilns - East Lomond

The massive stone limekilns are very well preserved considering their exposed location, while the pools nearby are all that remains of the quarry. Lead and silver were also to be found in these hills, and in the 1850's a rumour spread that gold had been found on West Lomond and a short lived, and no doubt fruitless, gold-rush began.

*From the limekilns return to the main path and continue up East Lomond until you reach the remains of the ditch and rampart that mark the site of the outer defences of the **Iron Age Hillfort (3)**.*

Large scale hill forts of this kind date from the **Iron Age**, which began in Scotland some time around 200 BC. The exploitation of iron opened up new possibilities in both agriculture and warfare – land could now be ploughed or cleared for grazing, and better weapons could be made relatively cheaply. It was probably the advances in military hardware—such as the introduction of the chariot—that led to the need for more secure defences, such as hill forts; although these forts were only occupied for a relatively brief period. All were constructed sometime before 83 AD and probably not occupied after that date. Their occupants were mostly working farm-

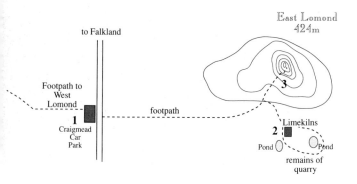

The Lomond Hills

ers and craftsmen, led by a chieftain, and the fort served as a fortified village.

East Lomond, at 424m the highest hill fort in Fife, retains only the ruins of its former defences, although one of its concentric rings of ditches and ramparts can still be seen. These ramparts were originally quite formidable, often including what **Julius Caesar** called the 'Murus Gallicus'—a vitrified stone wall. Archaeological evidence suggests that the outer defences of the fort may have been constructed much later than the rest—possibly in the Dark Ages, around 600-850AD.

From the top of the hill there are excellent views of the surrounding villages and across to West Lomond. When **Carlyle** visited the Lomond Hills in 1816, he described the view of Falkland as 'like a black old bit of coffin or protrusive piece of shinbone striking through the soil of the dead past.'

Return to the car park by the same route. From the car park there is a clearly marked path to ***West Lomond***.

Half way between East and West Lomond is **Maiden Castle,** another hill fort of indeterminate age on a low hillock. The remains of a ditch and rampart can be seen, while further up the slope are faint traces of the inner defensive lines.

20

HILL OF TARVIT

The House
Gardens
Laundry
Hill Walk
Scotstarvit Tower

Starting point: Hill of Tarvit

Directions to Start
A91 to Cupar, then A92 south from Cupar
to the A916. Signposted.

Opening times
Open at Easter, then
May 1st to end of October 2-6pm.
Closed during the winter.

Recommended Map
Ordnance Survey Landranger 59

Tearoom
Hill of Tarvit

Only one family ever lived at **Hill of Tarvit**, and theirs is a story of triumph and tragedy. The house was built by **Robert Lorimer** in 1906 for **Frederick Bower Sharp** (1862-1932), whose father, a Dundee 'Jute Prince', had left £750,000 in his will when he died in 1895—a fortune based on deals such as the sale of sandbags to both the Union and the Confederacy during the American Civil War.

Frederick Sharp made his own fortune as a financier and director of the London Midland and Scottish Railway, and was an extremely astute art collector. Hill of Tarvit was designed to house the art collection he had built up over the years.

Frederick Sharp was also a keen golfer, he was a member of the **Royal and Ancient** at St Andrews, and he had a golf course laid out in front of the house just beyond the present terracing. Local people were allowed to use it, but it was ploughed up during the Second World War.

When Frederick Sharp died in 1932 he was succeeded by his only son, **Hugh Sharp** (1897-1937). Hugh had led what seemed to be an almost perfect life—Oxford, distinguished service in World War One (including an MC and bar, several Mentions-in-Dispatches, the Croix de Guerre and the Italian Award for Valour), and a successful career in the city—until tragedy struck in the winter of 1937.

Hugh had recently become engaged and was intending to visit his fiance in Glasgow. Because of the bad weather, she suggested he should travel by rail rather than by road. The train Hugh caught was involved in a disastrous accident at Castlecary near Falkirk. Two trains collided injuring nearly 200 people. Hugh Sharp was one of 35 unfortunate people who lost their lives.

Hugh's sister, Elisabeth, continued to live at Hill of Tarvit with her mother, but Mrs Sharp died in 1946 and Elisabeth sadly died of cancer only two years later aged 38. It was only 42 years since the house had been built. The estate and Frederick Sharp's art collection were left to the National Trust for Scotland, who have taken great care in restoring the house to its original state.

The house itself replaced an earlier one, **Wemyss Hall**, that stood on this site. Wemyss Hall had been built here by **Sir William Bruce** in 1696; but only the Victorian servants quarters from that house were incorporated in Lorimer's design. The individual rooms of the house were designed by Lorimer to house specific treasures from Frederick Sharp's collection, and each reflected the different style of the objects on display.

The first room you come to is **The Hall**, designed in the Baronial style to show off the 16th century Flemish tapestries. It also contains a number of Chinese vases and bronzes.

*The doorway near the entrance hall leads into **The Drawing Room**.*

This room houses Frederick Sharp's collection of French furniture and is a delightful contrast to the rather dark panelling of the Hall. The plasterwork in this room is particularly fine, with delicate foliage, flowers and wreaths on the ceiling. Above the fireplace is a portrait of Hugh Sharp as a young boy dating from 1904.

Hill of Tarvit

*Leaving the drawing room, pass through the hall and the dining room passage to the **Dining Room**.*

The Dining Room was designed to display Sharp's collection of Georgian furniture, and the Lorimer plasterwork in this room is extremely elaborate. Near the window is a massive Brescia marble wine cooler, whilst the most noticeable feature of the dining table itself is the 19th century German silver galleon. Leading off the dining room are the well preserved service premises—the servery, the pantry and the kitchen. The white-tiled kitchen contains a large range and an extensive selection of copper pots and pans.

The Library is situated next to the dining room on the way back to the Hall. Decorated with Regency furniture, it also houses portraits by **Sir Henry Raeburn** and **Allan Ramsay**. Just beside the door there is a beautiful wooden box, inlaid with a depiction of ships under full sail.

Go back to the hall and up the staircase to the first floor.

On this floor the main rooms open to the public are the south west bedroom, with its adjoining dressing room and ante room, and the bathroom. The main bedroom has an unusual domed ceiling—ask the guide about the extraordinary echo—and the bathroom has a remarkable shower system, not to mention a lavatory designed by Lorimer and bearing his plumbing *nom de plume* 'Remirol'.

Throughout the house you will find the guides extremely friendly and helpful, and it is well worth taking advantage of their expertise. Finally, do not leave the house without visiting the excellent tea-room.

> *On leaving the house, walk through the garden at the rear and go through the massive wrought iron gates, made by Thomas Hadden of Edinburgh, onto the path that leads up the hill.*

From the top of the hill there are fine views of virtually the whole of Fife. The monument that stands on top of the hill was placed here in 1897 to mark the Diamond Jubilee of Queen Victoria. It replaced Cupar's Market Cross which had been sited here in the 19th century by a member of the Wemyss family who had won it from the Provost of Cupar. The cross was eventually returned to Cupar.

Scotstarvit Tower

The key to Scotstarvit Tower can be obtained from Hill of Tarvit, although you will be asked for a deposit. The Tower itself is situated just off the main road down the farm track opposite the entrance to Hill of Tarvit.

Built between 1550 and 1579, Scotstarvit is one of the best preserved towerhouses in Scotland. It was purchased by **Sir John Scot** in 1611 and it derives its name from him.

Sir John Scot was knighted in 1617 and became a Lord of Session in 1632. He was active in both politics and academic research, although his political ambitions were thwarted when he lost the hereditary office of Director of Chancery during the Commonwealth and failed to retrieve it after the restoration of **Charles II**. His disappointment caused him to write the curiously titled *Staggering State of Scots Scotsmen*; but he went on to found the chair of Latin at St Andrews and helped finance the work of the famous cartographer **John Blaeu**.

> 'At length our Scotland presents itself to the world. It will now hold an honourable place among the other countries of the earth in the grand and celebrated Atlas of Monsieur John Blaeu, to which the world has seen nothing comparable.'
> **Gordon of Straloch**
> *Letter to Sir John Scot*
> *24th January 1648*

The design of the tower itself is extremely simple, with a rectangular main block and a turnpike stair at one corner. It originally had three chambers, divided into six rooms. The first floor housed the hall, which would have been the most important room in the Tower, and which still retains its three stone window seats. Above the hall was the Laird's room, and at the very top of the tower was the attic, which may have been Sir John Scot's study. The fireplace from the attic, dated 1627 and bearing the initials of Sir John and his wife Anne Drummond, is now in the smoking room at Hill of Tarvit.

You can go out onto the parapet where you will see the unusual stone cap-house of the turnpike stair.

21
DAIRSIE CASTLE
AND RIVERSIDE WALK

Dairsie Bridge
St Mary's Church
Dairsie Castle
River Eden

Starting Point : St Mary's Church

Directions to start: Follow the B939 west from St
Andrews and take the right turn for
Strathkinness. Continue straight on at the cross-
roads in Strathkinness, and about 2 miles down
this road you will come to Dairsie Bridge. Cross
the bridge and turn left for St Mary's Church.

Recommended Map
Ordnance Survey Landranger 59

Distance: 1 mile

St Mary's Old Parish Church (1) is situated on rising ground overlooking the River Eden. Dating from 1621, it was built by Archbishop Spottiswoode of St Andrews whose arms and initials can be seen above the door.

After the signing of the **National Covenant** in February 1638, Spottiswoode fell foul of the covenanters and was accused of 'profaning the Sabbath, carding and dicing, riding through the country the whole day, tippling and drinking in taverns till midnight' as well as virtually anything else that sprang to mind. Whether or not he was guilty, Spottiswoode was hounded out of office and died in London in 1639. He was buried in Westminster Abbey. His son, Sir Robert Spottiswoode, was also to suffer at the hands of the covenanters, after being taken prisoner at the Battle of Philiphaugh in 1645.

The **Battle of Philiphaugh** was fought on 12th September 1645 between the Royalist forces of **Montrose** and the covenanting forces of **David Leslie** at the junction of the Yarrow and Ettrick rivers near Selkirk. Montrose was defeated and forced to flee north to the Highlands, eventually escaping to Norway. Many of his comrades were less fortunate: most of his Irish troops and their camp-followers were massacred in the courtyard of **Newark Castle** just south west of the battlefield, while Spottiswoode and several other high-ranking prisoners were beheaded at the Market Cross in St Andrews in January 1646.

The most notable feature of the church is its strange octagonal belfry and stone spire. Originally, the church had a flat roof, but this was replaced by the present one in the late 18th century.

Leave the churchyard by the north east gate and follow the path around to the castle.

The ruins of **Dairsie Castle (2)** lie just to the south west of the church. This is the second castle to have been built on this spot, the previous one having been occupied by **King David II** in the middle of the 14th century. One of the few Parliaments ever held in Fife took place here in 1335. At one stage the castle was occupied by the Learmonth family, who were, apparently, ancestors of the Russian writer Lermontov.

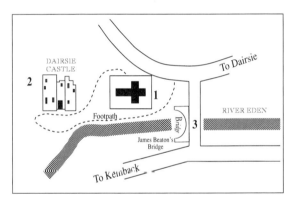

Like the church, the present castle was built during the time of Archbishop Spottiswoode and although originally quite a substantial tower house, only the north and south walls are still standing. The rest consists largely of heaps of rubble that litter what was once the interior of the castle. The south west tower, however, retains some of its corbelling, despite an enormous crack in the stonework that splits the tower from top to bottom. This tower also retains the gunholes which are usually seen in castles of this period.

Follow the path that leads past this tower and

descends towards the riverbank. This path leads across a wooden footbridge to the Eden, eventually bringing you back to the field below the church.

Down to the right is **Dairsie Bridge (3)**, which dates from about 1530 and has the arms of **Archbishop James Beaton** of St Andrews (c.1480-1539), on the east side. Turn left here, head for the gate that leads onto the road just in front of the church, and you are back at the starting point.

22

THE ISLE OF MAY

Cluniac Chapel
The May Beacon
Stevenson Lighthouse
Nature Reserve

Starting Point: Anstruther

Details of sailings can be obtained from the
Tourist Information Centres at Anstruther (0333
311073) and St Andrews (0334 72021), or from Mr
J. Reaper (0333 310103) and it is advisable to book
in advance. The crossing is about 5 miles and
waterproofs are essential.

Opening Times
Summer only

Recommended Map
Ordnance Survey Landranger 59

St Adrian is supposed to have lived on the Isle of May and to have been killed there by Viking raiders sometime around 875. A Benedictine Abbey was established on the island in the middle of the 12th century, although by the 14th century the monks were forced to seek refuge from persistent raiders, and moved to the Priory in Pittenweem. The island was visited by James IV in the 1490's and by James V in 1540. By 1549 it was in the possession of Patrick Learmonth of Dairsie; although he considered it of little value, as its only asset—its rabbit population—had been more or less wiped out as a result of English attacks.

The ownership of the island passed through many hands, until it was eventually bought by the Commissioners for Northern Lights for £60,000 from **Henrietta, Duchess of Portland**, the daughter of **General Scott of Balcomie** *(see Kilrenny Walk)* who had owned it since the 1760's.

After 1815, the main importance of the island was as the site of various lighthouses. The monks of the 12th century abbey may have kept lights burning to aid pilgrims crossing the Forth; but the first real light was established in the squat tower in the centre of the island by **Alexander Cunningham** and **James Maxwell** in the 1630's—they charged passing ships for the maintenance of the light: foreign ships paid four shillings a ton, Scottish ships paid two shillings. This early light was really just a giant brazier, burning coal on a massive grate at the top of the tower. As much as four tons of coal were sometimes consumed in one night.

This primitive arrangement had its dangers—in 1791 George Anderson, the keeper, and his family

The Isle of May

were suffocated in the lighthouse by fumes from the ashes that had accumulated around the building—but it persisted until the beginning of the 19th century, when a new lighthouse was built by **Robert Stevenson**—a lighthouse that still functions today. This lighthouse was continually modified as the technology developed—cylindrical lenses were introduced in the 1830's, and electric lighting was installed in 1886.

The Isle of May Lighthouse, like almost all Britain's lighthouses, is now automatic, and the Northern Lighthouse Board sold the island to the Nature Conservancy Council in 1989.

There have been many wrecks around the Isle of May, but the one that occurred in July 1837, when an excursion boat, the *Johns* from Cellardyke, with 65 people on board was wrecked at Kirkhaven, was particularly tragic. This is George Gourlay's description of that day:

> 'It is a summer day and a summer sea, and the island is reached betimes, and with Kirkonhaven on the lea the boat is steered for the little pier. The breakers, the last echo of the sea winds, are white and booming on the reef; but the oarsmen are young and fearless, and a skilful hand is on the helm, and all goes well. "A good voyage, and a pleasant landing," cries one; but at that very moment a wild plunge and a startled cry betrays the danger – scarcely heard, however, when, with a deafening crash, the doomed boat falls upon the skerry.'

George Gourlay
Memorials of Cellardyke

Thirteen people were lost and the owner of the boat, John Sutherland was charged with culpable homicide, largely because he had allowed 65 people onto a boat only 36ft long and 12ft wide. He was acquitted.

During the **First World War**, when much of the British Grand Fleet was stationed at Rosyth, its key position at the mouth of the river meant that the island was a vital link in the defences of the Forth, a role it was to play again, especially in the anti-submarine campaign during the Second World War. Aircraft from **HMS Jackdaw**, the airfield just outside Crail, practised low-level torpedo bombing close to the island and quite a few aircrew lost their lives in the process. They are remembered in a display in Crail Museum and some of them are buried in the modern extension to Crail Churchyard.

The Isle of May is now a nature reserve and bird sanctuary, and all manner of seabirds can be seen along its precipitous cliffs—puffins, guillemots, razorbills, and kittiwakes all nest here in fairly large numbers. Boat trips leave regularly from Anstruther and Crail from Easter to October—weather and tides permitting.

Notes

Notes

Notes

Notes

Notes

Notes

Notes

Notes